AMERICAN HORTICULTURAL SOCIETY
PRACTICAL GUIDES

CONTAINERS

AMERICAN HORTICULTURAL SOCIETY
PRACTICAL GUIDES

CONTAINERS

PETER ROBINSON

DK PUBLISHING, INC.
www.dk.com.

A DK PUBLISHING BOOK
www.dk.com

PROJECT EDITOR Samantha Gray
ART EDITOR Rachael Parfitt

SERIES EDITOR Pamela Brown
SERIES ART EDITOR Stephen Josland
US EDITOR Ray Rogers

MANAGING EDITOR Louise Abbott
MANAGING ART EDITOR Lee Griffiths

DTP DESIGNER Matthew Greenfield

PRODUCTION MANAGER Patricia Harrington

First American Edition, 1999
4 6 8 10 9 7 5

Published in the United States by
DK Publishing, Inc.,375 Hudson Street, New York, New York 10014

Library of Congress Cataloging-in-Publication Data

Containers. -- 1st American ed.
      p.   cm.   --   (AHS practical guides)
Includes index.
ISBN 0–7894–4152–7 (alk. paper)
1. Container gardening. 2. Plant containers
I. DK Publishing, Inc. II. Series.
SB418.P58 1999
635.9'86--dc21   98–41492
                                        CIP

Reproduced by Colourscan, Singapore
Printed and bound by Star Standard Industries, Singapore

CONTENTS

GARDENING IN CONTAINERS *7*

Choosing from the wide range of containers and the
merits of different materials; which plants to put in them;
and ideas for putting on a good display.

CREATIVE IDEAS FOR CONTAINERS *23*

PLANTING AND ROUTINE CARE *54*

Which soil mix to use; planting and looking after
containers throughout the year; training standards,
cones, and topiary animals.

GOOD PLANTS FOR CONTAINERS *64*

A guide to some of the best plants to grow as specimen
trees and shrubs, in mixed plantings and group displays
and in troughs, plus some easy edible plants.

GARDENING IN CONTAINERS

WHY CONTAINERS?

THERE CAN SCARCELY BE A YARD, balcony, or garden, however big or small, that would not benefit from a container or two. Brimming with flowers or refreshing greenery, windowboxes, pots, and planters help soften hard landscapes dominated by bricks and concrete. They create leafy pools of interest outside back doors and windows and bring color and scent to patios and terraces, making them perfect places to relax and unwind.

CREATIVE BEGINNINGS

Just one striking plant in a single pot will brighten a windowsill or the corner of a yard, but a stylized line of matching plants or cascading mixture of flowers and foliage has real impact. Grouping plants in separate pots is the easiest way to create a display. You can tend to each plant's individual needs, varying watering and feeding programs, adding and subtracting plants, and using different types of soil mix (see p.55). Mixed arrangements in large planters need more forethought but offer creative scope. Soil mix dries out less quickly in big pots, but it is essential that all the plants share similar requirements for shade or sun, water and food, and grow at a similar pace if one is not to overrun the others.

◄ LAYERED EFFECT
A tiered arrangement that includes fuchsias, nasturtiums, begonias, and geraniums makes maximum use of the space beneath a window. Staging can be bought already made; a lower display could easily be built up on stacked bricks.

▶ INSTANT SUNSHINE
A regimented row of dwarf sunflowers perks up a plain brick wall, albeit for a limited period.

CHOOSING CONTAINERS

Any container needs to be practical as well as decorative, so it is important to consider materials along with size, site, and style when making your choice. It also helps if you know what you want to grow in it. The most successful combinations are those where plants suit their container and both

> **Wooden containers must be treated with a weatherproof preservative**

container and plants suit their setting. Aim to choose a style that blends with your house and garden, outdoor furniture, and the surfaces, be they concrete, gravel, wooden decking, or brick.

Terracotta harmonizes easily and develops an attractive weathered look (this can be speeded up by coating the outside of new pots with yogurt to foster growth of algae and lichens). In warm weather, it tends to keep plant roots a little cooler than plastic. On the minus side, large pots are heavy to move once planted and are expensive.

Terracotta is breakable and can crack in winter (if this happens, a band of wire under the rim, twisted tight with pliers, usually keeps the pot in one piece and still functional). Since it is porous, clay will draw moisture from the soil mix, which then evaporates from the outside of the pot; soaking new pots before planting reduces the problem. Plastic, on the other hand, is light, durable, and inexpensive, but tall plants can make pots unstable. The soil mix, however, is less inclined to dry out.

FOLIAGE EFFECT
The aeonium (right), adds an architectural dimension to a garden setting in summer. In cold areas it would need moving into a greenhouse or conservatory for winter. Conversely, the ornamental kale (below), with its matching pot, should enliven a dull corner from autumn into the new year.

SUBTLE OR BOLD

Wood generally goes well with both plants and surroundings. It needs to be treated with a waterproof preservative in a natural shade or in one of the attractive colors now available (*see p.33*). You can line the inside with plastic, punctured with drainage holes, or stand a plastic pot or trough inside. All containers should be raised off the ground on feet or blocks to allow water to drain; this is especially important for wood to prevent the base from rotting.

Small trees and tall shrubs need sturdy, stable containers. Reconstituted stone pots are among the heaviest. If plants are tender and need moving into a greenhouse or conservatory for winter, use a trolley or a board fitted with wheels to move them.

Some of the cheaper, less attractive materials, or maybe containers that have passed their prime, can be transformed quickly and easily with a couple of coats of paint, a simple stencil, or a mosaic of broken tiles (*see Creative Ideas, pp.25–29*). If you use strong colors, choose suitably bold plants that won't be outshined by their container.

▲ TIME FOR MOSAIC
The rather tender lavender, L. stoechas, *is a good match for this mosaic pot. Hardier 'Hidcote' would make a suitable alternative.*

▼ VALUABLE GREENERY
A classic example of the value of containers in an enclosed space without soil. Almost every bit of wall and floor is put to good use.

SITING AND GROUPING CONTAINERS

CONTAINERS GIVE YOU THE OPPORTUNITY to combine contrasting plants in a small area. Group displays extend the options because you can use plants that have different soil mix, watering, and feeding needs. To emphasize contrast in foliage form, opt for containers of a similar material and color. Single architectural specimens look best set apart. Use them as a focal point in the center of a courtyard or to draw the eye to the end of a path or lawn.

RIGHT PLANT, RIGHT PLACE

Placing and arranging container plants needs the same sort of care that you would give to planting a bed or border. Plants in pots are more exposed to extremes of weather than those growing in the ground; their roots may overheat in summer or freeze in winter. In cold areas, be prepared to give plants that are not fully hardy winter protection (*see p.59*); in summer, the outer pots in a group will help keep the inner ones cooler. For hot sites, choose plants that grow well in dry conditions, usually those with spiky or needlelike, furry or waxy, often gray leaves.

Flowers in strong primary colors, particularly reds, are most effective in strong light; pastel shades are often best kept away from full sun. Foliage color is also affected by light intensity. Many variegated plants need sunshine to bring out the best coloration in their leaves.

FOCAL POINT
A spiky cordyline ends a vista. Make planting easy by using a plastic pot in the top of a decorative jar, with some stones in the base to keep it stable. This makes the plant easy to move.

FRAGRANT REWARDS

Growing scented and aromatic plants in containers means that you can place them in just the right spot to appreciate them, near tables and chairs, for instance, or immediately by a door. In small courtyard areas, scents linger on warm afternoons and evenings, increasing the pleasure of sitting, eating, and drinking outdoors.

Lilies make splendid container plants, but, if scent is important, check before you buy, since some have little or no fragrance.

> On summer evenings, the scent from windowsill plants can waft indoors

Heliotrope and dwarf flowering tobacco (*Nicotiana*) are suitable for windowboxes, along with aromatic herbs such as thyme and marjoram. Shrubs provide some of the finest scents. For an exotic touch, angels' trumpets (*Brugmansia*) are hard to rival in summer, while the leaves of evergreen rosemary, lavender, and myrtle remain aromatic all year. Place them where you can brush past and catch the benefit. Given the support of a tepee of stakes, shrub stems, or a wire or trellis obelisk, flowering vines can be grown in a large pot. They will need frequent watering and regular feeding.

▲ GROUP STRATEGY
The introduction of containerized grasses as a foreground to the broad-leaved hostas creates a display based on contrasting foliage shapes.

▼ COURTYARD COMPOSITION
The gentle colors of the tulips, pansies, and geraniums and the natural textures of the trough and pots both harmonize with and enhance the backdrop of a gray stone wall.

MATCHING PLANTS WITH POTS

THERE IS AN ENORMOUS RANGE OF PLANTS that can be grown in containers, from summer bedding to small trees, provided the container is stable and there is room for plant roots. Containers enable you to grow plants that would not survive in your garden soil: rhododendrons, for example, which need acidic conditions. In a barrel you can use acidic soil mix. It is easy, too, to improve drainage with extra grit for rock garden plants and Mediterranean herbs.

STYLE AND PURPOSE

Take advantage of a plant's natural habit of growth when matching it with its container. Give a trailing plant sufficient height to spill over the sides. Tall pots and urns are ideal. Alternatively, stand a smaller pot on a small stack of bricks or another upturned pot. Most group displays are improved if you can set some of the plants at different levels. Trailing fuchsias, helichrysums, nasturtiums, and lobelias can all be put to good use. These are also the sort of plants you need to soften the edges of a mixed planting in a large container. A mixture of different habits – upright and bushy, trailing or spreading – make any display more interesting whether planted in one or several separate containers.

Rock garden plants, small bulbs, and carpeting herbs such as thymes generally do not need deep root runs and are good in shallow pots. Sempervivums will thrive and multiply in as little as 1–2in/2.5–5cm of soil.

Balance is all important. Think about the shape any plant will develop when teaming it with its container. Too small a plant in too large a pot is likely to look silly. It is also unwise to give a plant more soil mix than its roots can possibly reach and which may become sodden and sour. While waiting for a newly planted shrub to grow to its full size, fill the space in a large container with annuals such as impatiens, petunias, pansies, and lobelias. Or better still, pot the shrub on, year after year, gradually increasing the pot's size.

THE SHAPE OF THINGS
The garden, right, constructed entirely of raised beds and containers on different levels makes a fine setting for spiky foliage plants and trailing creepers. Similarly, a simple but stylish pot emphasizes the neat pincushion shape of the saxifrage below.

◀ CUTTING EDGE
Boxwood has been cleverly clipped into shapes that work well with their containers. Choose containers with uniform, muted colors and textures that do not detract from the topiary.

▼ FLORA AND FAUNA
Characterful birds and other animals can be created by training small-leaved ivies around a wire frame (see p.62). The results are more rapid than by clipping boxwood or yew.

THINKING BIG

For trees and shrubs that will be an important part of the scene for many years, perhaps the backbone of a grouping or a specimen displayed in splendid isolation, it is often worth investing in an especially attractive planter or pot. Some plants and

> Topiary that needs years of dedicated clipping deserves a great pot

containers make obvious partners. Beautiful glazed ceramic pots are perfect for Oriental-looking trees and shrubs such as Japanese maples, bamboos, and rhododendrons.

Unfortunately, the more valuable the pot (and its plant) the greater the chance of it being stolen, so you may need to think about some form of security, such as threading a chain through the drainage hole and padlocking it to a post or railing, or even cementing the pot in place.

IDEAS FOR IMPROVISATION

THERE ARE MANY ALTERNATIVES to using specifically made containers for plants. Virtually any object that can hold soil mix and be adapted with drainage holes may be transformed into a plant pot. Chimney pots, wicker baskets, hollowed-out tree trunks, waterproof boots, wheelbarrows, ceramic sinks, galvanized buckets, and old bird cages are in many cases not as costly as store-bought containers and will add a sense of originality to your garden.

CHARACTERFUL CONTAINERS

Chimney pots are particularly useful for introducing height to a container grouping. Their narrow shape also makes them very suitable for limited spaces. Instead of filling the entire depth with soil mix, insert a smaller pot in the top, as for the decorative jar (*see p.10*), supporting it if necessary by partially filling the chimney pot with bricks or stones. Alternatively, fill the chimney pot to half its depth with a good drainage material, such as gravel or small stones

with pea gravel in between, then add soil mix to just below the rim. Tall containers, including chimney pots and galvanized metal florists' buckets, look best displaying plants such as trailing fuchsias or petunias, which can spill attractively down the sides.

If you are inventive, you can also make decorative containers from inexpensive salvage materials, such as ceramic tiles, terracotta ridging tiles, or large terracotta drainpipes. You may have such materials left over from building projects, or you can

▶ CHIMNEY POT DISPLAY
A chimney pot is an ideal container for the tender fuchsia 'Annabel', which must be moved to a frost-free place in winter.

▼ CONTAINERS FROM CLAY TILES
Containers made from sections of clay tiles combine subtle colors that offset the vibrant geranium blooms.

Soil mix, placed in a smaller pot or over a base layer of drainage material, fills only the upper part of the chimney pot

An underplanting of *Lobelia erinus* 'White Cascade' trails over the edges of the pot

◀ VEGETABLE RACK
*A vegetable rack
lined with moss and
an inner layer of
plastic provides ample
space for soil mix in
which to grow plants,
here including dark-
leaved basil, thyme,
curled parsley, and
scented geraniums.*

▼ HOLLOW LOG
*A contrast in color
and habit is provided
by* Heuchera
'Palace Purple' *and*
Dryopteris *planted in
a hollowed-out log.
Make sure that there
are drainage holes in
the base of the
container.*

obtain them inexpensively from a salvage
yard. Where necessary, join pieces together
with mortar, making sure that any large
area of mortar is inside the container.

All sorts of objects can make surprisingly
effective containers. For example, a vegetable
rack can be lined with moss with an inner

Make sure that all improvised containers have drainage holes

layer of plastic. Cut holes in the base of the
plastic for drainage, then make slits in the
sides through which you can insert young
plants in the same way as planting up a
hanging basket. A hollowed-out tree trunk
can be turned into an attractive container, or
pieces of bark-covered lumber can be nailed
together to make a trough. Stand wooden
containers on wedges and use a soil mix
that allows rapid drainage (*see pp.54–55*).

TREES, SHRUBS, AND CLIMBERS

GROWING WOODY PLANTS IN CONTAINERS gives a sense of permanence and structure to a paved area, while the plants themselves can influence the style of the garden, creating a formal, informal, or even subtropical effect. By matching an elegantly shaped or handsomely textured container with a boldly sculptural small tree or shrub, you can create a stunning focal point. The range of plants you can grow is increased if you give them appropriate protection in winter.

SCREENING AND PRIVACY

Evergreen trees, shrubs, and climbers grown in containers will soften the appearance of walls, fences, and other hard surfaces all year round and help increase privacy.

For sculptural form, grow evergreens with boldly shaped leaves, such as × *Fatshedera lizei*, fatsia, palmlike cordylines, and *Cycas* *revoluta*. Exotic and eye-catching, they all need careful placing and, in most climates, will need to be moved into a greenhouse or conservatory for winter. In enclosed city gardens you may want to increase the sense of light and air with a delicate-leaved Japanese maple (*Acer palmatum*) or a cutleaf buckthorn.

A CORNER DISPLAY
The catkins of this Kilmarnock willow (Salix caprea 'Kilmarnock') *appear like large droplets from a fountain over the cool blue container and the underplanting of* Helleborus argutifolius. *Surrounding the container are* Helleborus foetidus, *the striking foliage of* Arum italicum, *and a hebe, bringing this sheltered corner to life in late winter.*

A PERFECT MATCH
*The Oriental effect of
this blue-glazed
container and the
pebble mulch
complement the
purple-leaved
Japanese maple. The
pebbles have practical
value as well, keeping
the roots shaded and
cool and helping to
conserve moisture.*

COLOR AND SCENT

One of the pleasures of container planting is the ease with which you can introduce flower or foliage color to areas that might otherwise lack interest. Silver-leaved shrubs, such as *Convolvulus cneorum*, help cool down sunny patios, and both foliage and flowers of a variegated abutilon have a refreshing quality. Make the most of trees and shrubs with scented flowers or leaves – lavender and rosemary, for instance – by siting them near a sitting area. Since this is likely to be the most sheltered part of the garden, it will also be good for myrtle and bay, which both need protection from strong winds, which can damage their leaves.

YEAR-ROUND INTEREST

Many sculptural plants look even more effective in winter than during the summer, for example the formal contours of a geometrically clipped boxwood (*Buxus*) or yew (*Taxus*). Japanese maples come into their own again at this time of year with their exquisite tracery of fine branches, and the bare twisting stems of the corkscrew hazel, *Corylus avellana* 'Contorta', and *Salix* 'Erythroflexuosa' also have great impact when they are grown in containers. Ivies, such as yellow-variegated 'Goldheart' or curly-leaved 'Cristata', can be used to enliven gloomy corners or camouflage unsightly vertical surfaces. In summer,

> ### Balance tall trees and shrubs with handsome, sturdy containers

some forms of greenery can be just as interesting as flowers. Try introducing some sound with the gentle rustle of a bamboo such as *Sasa palmata* f. *nebulosa*. Given a reasonably sheltered spot, its broad, glossy leaves can look splendid all year.

FLOWERS FOR CONTAINERS

MAKE THE MOST OF THE WONDERFUL RANGE of tender perennials and annuals that actually thrive in strong sunlight to bring flower color to parts of the garden where woody plants would soon show signs of suffering. By contrast, the deep shade caused by buildings or high fences can be perfect for many herbaceous perennials, and for many lilies. Use bulbs, such as small daffodils and crocus or bright tulips, to extend the flowering season in spring and autumn.

EXUBERANT DISPLAYS

The ever-expanding range of summer bedding offered as small plantlets or plugs in garden centers and catalogs makes it easy to put together stunning combinations without the bother of sowing seed, pricking out, and hardening off. Some of these plants have been bred specifically for container-

▲ HOT COLORS FOR A SUNNY SITE
A terracotta pot holds a vibrant display of red-and gold-flowering plants, including cosmos, Rudbeckia *'Rustic Dwarfs' and 'Marmalade',* helichrysum, *and* Santolina chamaecyparissus.

growing and are both compact and free-flowering. Although often offered in early spring, buy them early only if you have a greenhouse where you can grow them on. Do not be tempted to plant them outside until all danger of frost is past.

For continuous flowering, deadhead plants regularly and feed occasionally with a high-potassium fertilizer such as tomato fertilizer. A lot of annuals and bedding plants, including gerberas, geraniums, osteospermums, and salvias, need sun to produce their best flowers, but lobelia, impatiens, *Begonia semperflorens*, pansies, and flowering tobacco (*Nicotiana*) all

---

Trailing lobelias create a curtain of flowering stems for a windowbox

---

flower well in light shade. For a plant that will flower through dull, damp periods, petunias make the best choice, with a wide range of flower colors – hot or cool, dashingly striped or prettily veined.

PERENNIALS FOR POTS

Use large barrels to group perennials or, easier to arrange, plant them singly in smaller containers. Striking single plantings include agapanthus, with elegant large blue or white flowerheads, and variegated hostas for decorative foliage and flowers.

Many herbaceous perennials, particularly woodland species such as heucheras and

▲ PORTABLE PLANTS
Small containers allow you to move plants such as tender Eucomis bicolor *outside in summer, then back indoors for winter protection.*

◀ SIMPLE BUT DRAMATIC
A group of variegated 'Keizerskroon' tulips shows the impact that can be made by planting a single variety.

tiarellas, are shade tolerant. Set them off with perennial foliage plants with a distinctive shape and growth habit, such as ornamental grasses and ferns, which thrive in shade. Most perennials provide summer interest only, but there are a few exceptions, such as liriope and bergenia, with evergreen foliage as well as attractive flowers in autumn and spring respectively.

Best Ways for Growing Bulbs
In large containers, bulbs can be planted in layers (*see p.57*), with annuals growing above for instant color. Often, however, they are best grown in a container of their own. Tulips, for instance, make a striking display; in pots they are best grown for one season only and then planted in the garden after flowering, if possible. Lilies are irresistible and make excellent container plants, but their displays are brief and they, too, are best grown in separate pots.

▲ COOL WHITES TO THRIVE IN SUNSHINE
This sun-loving mixture of white petunias and Helichrysum *'Roundabout' takes on a luminous quality in dusky evening light.*

Fruit, Vegetables, and Herbs

MOST HERBS MAKE IDEAL CONTAINER PLANTS, their aromatic leaves scenting windowsills and patios (*see p.22*). Fruit and vegetables demand time and care, requiring regular watering and feeding – a liquid fertilizer is easiest to apply. You will never produce mammoth crops, but at least they can go straight from plant to plate. In cool climates, citrus trees will be ornamental rather than productive; looseleaf lettuce or tiers of ripening strawberries will fulfill both roles.

Fruit in Containers

Fruit in containers can be included in an ornamental garden design more easily than vegetables. In a sunny courtyard or patio, you can create a Mediterranean effect by growing figs and citrus trees in pots, although they may need to be protected in winter in a greenhouse or conservatory.

Consider what types of containers will best suit what you want to grow. Fruit trees need large containers that can hold enough soil mix to act as a buffer for roots in dry conditions. Strawberry jars look decorative and are a space-saving way to grow strawberry plants, provided all the fruit

> On a patio, you may get to the strawberry crop before the birds

receives sufficient sun to ripen. You may need to turn the pot from time to time. Tiny alpine strawberries do well in light shade and provide small but delicious pickings. Add coarse sand to the soil mix for strawberries, especially in the tiered, specifically designed pots, to aid water penetration. Regular watering is essential while fruit is developing.

Vegetables in Containers

The best vegetables for containers are shallow-rooted, compact, quick-maturing varieties. To create a mini-potager effect, plant more than one type of vegetable in a

MEDITERRANEAN-STYLE CITRUS
A lemon tree growing in an elegant terracotta pot looks wonderful on a sunny patio. You may need to move it into a conservatory or greenhouse for protection in winter.

large container, combining, for instance, a frilly-leaved lettuce such as 'Lollo Rossa' with feathery-topped carrots. Growing a combination of plants can help ward off pests, which are less attracted to mixed scents than strong, single ones.

If you have a sunny, sheltered corner, it is fun to try some of the colorful varieties of eggplant and peppers. They are tender and need a long growing season to produce anything worthwhile, but many seed suppliers offer an exciting range, sometimes as small plants.

▲ A MINI-POTAGER
A wooden trough filled with a combination of red cabbages and nasturtiums creates a mini-potager effect and allows the occasional plundering of leaves for summer salads.

▼ STRAWBERRY CASCADE
Terracotta pots, built up one inside the other with room between for soil mix and roots, create planting tiers that can be filled with a mixture of herbs and alpine strawberries.

SUITABLE VEGETABLES

FOR SUN AND SHELTER

Eggplant Small-fruited types
Chili peppers Compact varieties
Tomatoes Fast-ripening, small-fruited types
Peppers Compact varieties

FOR LIGHT SHADE

Green beans Dwarf, can be purple-podded
Scarlet runner beans Need a large pot plus a tepee of stakes
Lettuce Decorative types
Carrots Short-rooted varieties

GROWING HERBS

The great advantage of planting herbs in pots is that you can position them in a convenient spot near to the house. Placing an herb container by the back door, for example, will allow you to water the plants and gather foliage easily.

Make sure that mixed species chosen for the same pot all enjoy the same conditions. Many herbs are of Mediterranean origin and require plenty of sunshine and good drainage to thrive and survive wet winters. Thyme, marjoram, rosemary, basil, bay, and sage all need sun, which also improves their flavor. Rosemary and bay need protection, too. Chives, parsley, chervil, and mint grow well in light shade; give mint a container of its own or it will overtake any neighbors. Suitable soil mixes include a soil/peat mix or a soilless mix. For Mediterranean herbs, add some sharp sand.

A mophead bay tree needs regular clipping, whether bought as a standard or trained from a small plant (see p.61)

◄ CULINARY TRIO
A standard bay tree with an underplanting of thyme and parsley provides the necessary ingredients for a "bouquet garni" to add piquancy to the cooking pot.

▲ AROMATIC ARRANGEMENT
A strawberry jar can be filled with attractive foliage herbs, such as purple and variegated sages, 'Silver Posie' thyme, and marjoram.

▼ PUNGENT PARTNERS
*A neat display combines basil and unrelated basil thyme (*Acinos arvensis*). Basil needs frequent harvesting, or stems become lanky.*

CREATIVE IDEAS FOR CONTAINERS

STENCILED MOTIF P.26

IT IS EASY TO TRANSFORM terracotta or plastic containers by decorating them with paint or stenciled patterns (*see pp.24–26*), perhaps to complement a color theme in your garden. For a really dazzling effect, cover pots with mosaic, using pieces of broken tile or even glass beads, pieces of mirror, or seashells (*see pp.27–29*). A windowbox provides welcome color through the seasons. Buy or make boxes to fit your windows perfectly and then use a paint finish, such as verdigris or crackle glaze, to give them the patina of age (*see pp.30–35*). Or, you may prefer to use wooden moldings to create a decorative paneled or ribbed effect (*see pp.36–37*). Before planting, it is important that the box is firmly secured to the sill (*see pp.38–39*). With a little woodworking skill, you can construct wooden planters that are both distinctive and stylish (*see pp.40–47*). Neither of the projects here requires specialized tools or tricky carpentry joins. Old stone troughs add a sense of time to a garden and form a pleasing setting for plants, but they are costly to buy. The solution is to make inexpensive faux troughs that are difficult to tell apart from the real thing. Two projects (*see pp.48–53*) show how to coat boxes with natural-looking hypertufa or an especially tough cement mix, which can be painted to give a contemporary look.

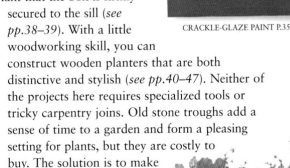

CRACKLE-GLAZE PAINT P.35

CLASSIC WOODEN PLANTER P.44

ALPINE TROUGH P.52

DECORATED POTS

FLOWERPOTS OF ALL SHAPES AND SIZES offer tremendous scope for adding decoration. Apply a colorwash to brighten a dull corner or stencil on shells or stars – whatever strikes your fancy and suits your planting design (*see next page*). Mosaic (*see p.27*) is more ambitious but looks superb teamed with dramatic yuccas and other bold foliage plants. You can transform utilitarian plastic and, now that factory-made terracotta has become so much more affordable, take the opportunity to experiment and make pots that are unique to your garden.

DISTRESSING TERRACOTTA

Give new terracotta pots a mellow, antique look by applying two colors, then rubbing patches of one away. Use water-based paint, preferably with a fairly chalky texture. The paints formulated for the distressed look and other special effects – often found in art or decorating shops – work well.

YOU NEED:

MATERIALS
• Terracotta pot
• Water-based paint in two colors
• Exterior matte varnish

TOOLS
• Paintbrush
• Steel wool in fine and coarse grades

TWO-COLOR EFFECT

1 Paint the pot with the first, base color, including inside the rim to just below the planting level. Allow to dry.

2 Apply the second color. You can water it down slightly over areas that are to be rubbed off in Step 3. Allow to dry.

3 Rub away some patches of the top coat of paint to reveal the base coat, using first coarse and then fine-grade steel wool. Blur edges as much as possible.

4 Brush off all dust, then apply a coat of exterior varnish for a weatherproof finish. Matte varnish loses its gloss when dry.

◄ SHADES OF SUMMER *Pinks, greens, and blues harmonize well with both foliage and flowers.*

STENCILING PATTERNS

If you are new to stenciling, choose a fairly simple motif, one that does not require intricate cutting out. The texture of clay provides an attractive background in itself, but a plastic pot, as shown below, needs to be painted first. When making the stencil, cut away all the excess cardboard so that you are left with a narrow border around the design. You can then stick the stencil closely to the pot and avoid spoiling the edge of the pattern.

USING SIMPLE MOTIFS

YOU NEED:

MATERIALS
- Flexible cardboard
- Clay flowerpot
- Latex or acrylic paint
- Scrap paper
- Exterior varnish

TOOLS
- Pencil
- Craft knife
- Masking tape
- Sponge
- Paintbrush

1 **Draw or trace** the design onto a piece of thin cardboard and carefully cut it out using a craft knife. Protect work surfaces.

2 **Stick the stencil** in place with the tape, stretching the stencil as taut as possible to prevent any paint from seeping underneath.

3 **Dab on the paint** using a sponge. Get rid of any excess paint first on some scrap paper. When dry, peel off the stencil (*see inset*) and varnish the pot, as on the previous page.

USING PLASTIC POTS

Apply an oil-based undercoat first to create a suitable surface for paint to adhere to, then a base coat of latex. Stencil on the motif in the same way as above, but remove the tape as gently as possible to avoid pulling off the base coat along with it. Varnish as before.

A seashell has been stenciled onto a base coat of slate blue. The rim is painted pink to match it

MAKING MOSAIC

Use mosaic to cover cheap or cracked terracotta or even thick, rigid plastic. The pattern can be as flamboyant or subtle as you want but, for a first attempt, avoid intricacy and choose the kind of random design shown here.

The spiky silhouette of *Yucca gloriosa* 'Variegata' suits the mosaic pattern

YOU NEED:

MATERIALS
- Flowerpot
- Drawing paper
- Tiles or old china
- Water-resistant combined tile adhesive and grout
- Latex or acrylic paint

TOOLS
- Ruler and pencil
- Hammer
- Cloth or newspaper
- Goggles
- Rubber gloves
- Tile nippers
- Tile file
- Putty knife
- Grout spreader
- Sponge
- Paintbrush

PLANT PARTNERS
Bold pots call for bold plants. Those with architectural shapes, such as this yucca, are ideal (take care: the leaves are very sharp). Phormiums, agaves, or succulents such as aeoniums would also be a good choice for a sunny corner. The shapes of these hot-climate plants suit the Mediterranean feeling of mosaic.

PLANNING THE DESIGN

1 **Measure and mark out** the shape of the pot, including the depth of the rim. You can do this in segments of halves or thirds.

2 **Place tiles between** cloth or paper to stop fragments from flying, then smash them with a hammer. For extra safety, wear goggles.

SHAPING AND ATTACHING THE PIECES

1 **Lay out the pieces** in your chosen pattern, using nippers to make the shapes and trim corners. Start from the top, laying pieces with a glazed edge at the rim for a smooth edge.

2 **Use a tile file** to remove any jagged edges and shape the pieces further. Keep your eyes protected with goggles while you are nipping or filing pieces of mosaic.

3 **Stick the mosaic pieces** onto the pot, smearing the undersides thickly with tile adhesive using a putty knife. Keep them in the arranged pattern as you transfer them one by one from paper to pot. Allow to set.

4 **Spread the grout** all over the surface of the mosaic, working it well into the joints between the pieces. Do not worry about getting it over the tiles – it will wipe off. (You can add colored dyes to the grout if you want it to blend or contrast with the mosaic.)

PRACTICAL TIPS

• Thin tiles are easiest to use. Keep to ceramics of an even thickness.
• Avoid tiles with a crackle glaze: they break with especially jagged edges.
• Keep the mosaic pieces fairly small.
• A combined adhesive/grout simplifies the job, but you can use separate formulations.

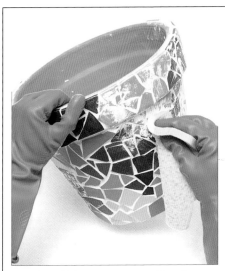

5 **Wipe off the excess grout** with a damp sponge or cloth before it hardens. When it has fully set, you can buff the surface of the mosaic using a dry sponge or cloth.

6 **Paint the inside rim,** using a color that suits the mosaic, to just below the soil level. This improves the finished look and hides any smudges of adhesive and grout.

ALTERNATIVE MATERIALS FOR MOSAICS

With a little inventiveness, all sorts of materials can be put to good use. Some will fare better than others in harsh weather. The glass tesserae, below right, made especially for mosaic, are frost-resistant. A coat of varnish will give shells a longer life.

◄ MIRROR
Rather than letting them bring you bad luck, use broken pieces to add a surreal touch, but handle them carefully.

GLASS NUGGETS ▶
These are sold for arranging in colored layers in jars, but they are excellent for mosaic work.

▼ TESSERAE
You can find a wide range of colors in craft shops and specialty mosaic suppliers.

▲ SHELLS
Give your beachcombing a new purpose. Sharp spirals and wavy scallop shapes add a geometric element as well as a marine look.

▲ BEADS
Ceramic or glass, small or large, use beads singly or in clusters to add interesting detail to a design.

WINDOWBOXES

A WINDOW WITHOUT A WINDOWBOX is a wasted opportunity for anyone who likes plants. Nor do the creative possibilities begin and end with deciding what to grow. The box itself can be decorated in many ways. Give it a rustic look or an air of urban sophistication with paint or ornamental wood finishes (*see pp.34–37*). Then, to create an effective planting design, experiment with combinations of upright and trailing plants and those with attractive foliage.

MAKING A WOODEN WINDOWBOX

Simple troughs made of weatherproofed wood can be planted up direct or used to hold pots. This windowbox has been designed for a 40×8in/100×20cm ledge, but the same method of construction can be used to suit any size. The bigger the box, the more securely it must be attached (*see pp.38–39*).

PRACTICAL TIPS

• If altering the dimensions of the box, make sure that it will still be deep enough for plant roots (for most plants, at least 8in/20cm).
• Smooth all rough-cut lumber edges with sandpaper before you start.
• When drilling, always put a scrap of wood underneath to protect the work surface.

YOU NEED:

MATERIALS

For this project, use wood of ¾in/2cm thickness. The lumber measurements are all for finished, planed wood.
• 2 side panels
38×7½in/96.5×19cm
• 2 end panels
6¾×6¾in/17×17cm
• Base 38×6¾in/96.5×17cm
• 30 2in/5cm screws plus a few extra
• Wood filler
• Your choice of materials to protect and decorate the box (*see pp.33–37*)

TOOLS

• Pencil
• Tape measure
• Drill, preferably electric
• ⅛in/4mm drill bit
• Countersink
• ½in/13mm drill bit, for drainage holes
• Screwdriver

POSITIONING THE END PANELS

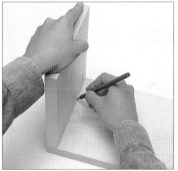

1 **Lay the base** flat on the workbench or table and, holding each of the small end panels in position against it, mark a line on the base along their inside edge.

2 **Mark, then drill** 3 evenly spaced holes for screws at each end of the base, using the ⅛in/4mm bit. Rest each end of the base on scraps of wood to keep it level and protect the work surface from the drill. Use a countersink (*see inset*) to make a shallow depression so that the screw head will lie just below the surface of the wood.

CONSTRUCTING THE BOX

3 **Screw one end** panel in place; you can use the other end panel, as here, for support. Screw the remaining end panel onto the other end of the base in the same way.

PRACTICAL TIPS

• For extra strength, glue joins with wood adhesive before screwing if you prefer, but this is not essential.

• When screwing one piece of wood to another, avoid any chance of the wood splitting by making a small "starter" hole in the second piece first, using an awl or a very fine drill.

4 **Lay each** of the side panels flat on the workbench in turn, and place the ends-and-base construction on them, marking around its inner edge.

5 **Mark screw positions** at equal intervals along the marked-off area, placing 3 up each of the side edges and 4 along the bottom edge. Bear in mind that the screws near the corners must be well clear of the joint.

6 **At each marked position,** drill and countersink screw holes on each of the long side panels. Screw the side panels to the base and end panels in order to complete the basic construction of the box.

HIDING SCREWS AND DRILLING DRAINAGE HOLES

2 **Turn the box** upside down and drill holes in the base for drainage, using the ½in/13mm bit. A box of these dimensions will need at least 6 holes.

1 **Fill in** the countersunk screw holes with wood filler to cover the screw heads. Make the filling slightly high, then sand it smooth and level when dry.

PROTECTING AND PRESERVING THE WOOD

Wood must be protected from the effects of damp soil mix within and rain and sun without, so it is essential to use an exterior-quality product to weatherproof it. Always treat both the inside and outside of any wooden container with preservative. You can use oil-based paint over primer, but it will need to be renewed regularly. More decorative paint finishes include crackle glaze and "verdigris" effects (*see next page*).

PRACTICAL TIPS

• For extra protection, line the inside with plastic punctured with drainage holes, or stand a plastic box inside to make it easy to change plantings whenever necessary.
• Stand the windowbox on wedges or feet so that water drains freely. Use a tray to catch surplus water and prevent it from dripping onto anything (or anybody) beneath.

BRIGHT HARMONY
Exterior preservatives, designed to let wood grain show through, come in an attractive range of soft colors as well as natural wood shades.

"FORGET-ME-NOT"   "IRIS BLUE"   "SAGE GREEN"   "SUNFLOWER"

Apply preservative evenly and, if possible, in the direction of the grain

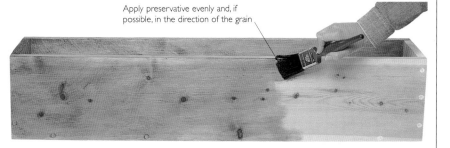

DECORATIVE PAINT FINISHES

It is easy to give a "designer" look to simple wooden containers by using craft paints to add color and texture. You can apply these paint finishes to any wooden container, including the planters on pages 40–47. Always apply clear exterior varnish over paint finishes to protect and seal them.

CREATING A VERDIGRIS EFFECT

YOU NEED:

MATERIALS
- Wood primer and undercoat, or an all-in-one product
- Olive green acrylic or latex paint
- Small jars of mint green, blue-green, and black acrylic paint
- Bronze or copper gilt cream
- Clear exterior matte varnish

TOOLS
- Paintbrush
- Stencil brush
- Scrap paper
- Brush cleaner

1 **Paint the bare wood** with primer and undercoat. Using an all-in-one, fast-drying product is a good way to save time.

2 **Apply an even coat** of olive green paint. Use long brush strokes and work in the same direction as the grain. Allow to dry.

3 **Dip the stencil brush** into the mint green paint and dab off the excess onto paper. Stipple on the color and allow to dry.

4 **Stipple on** the blue-green paint, applying it sparingly to create random concentrations of color. Allow the paint to dry.

5 **Mix some black paint** with the blue-green to make a dark shade. Use it to work in smudges of deeper color to create a naturalistic effect. Allow to dry.

6 **Apply tiny patches** of bronze or copper gilt cream with your fingertip. Seal with up to 3 coats of varnish. Give 2 coats of varnish to the inside of the box.

PRACTICAL TIPS

- Cover mistakes with undercoat and have another try.
- Choose good-quality brushes for the best finish.
- Most home supply stores stock a good selection of craft paints.

USING CRACKLE GLAZE

YOU NEED:

MATERIALS
• Wood primer and undercoat
• Base coat of acrylic paint (*here gold*)
• Crackle glaze
• Top coat of acrylic or latex paint (*here olive*)
• Clear exterior varnish, preferably with a matte or semigloss finish

TOOLS
• Paintbrush
• Brush cleaner

1 Prime and undercoat the wood, then brush on gold paint (*above*). Brush in the same direction as the wood grain and allow to dry.

2 Apply one thick coat or two thin coats of crackle glaze. (The top layer of paint will not crackle if there is not enough glaze.) Allow to dry.

3 Paint on a coat of olive green, using long, even brush strokes and keeping the brush loaded with plenty of paint. Allow to dry. As the paint dries it will shrink and crackle.

4 Apply up to 3 coats of exterior varnish to seal the paint and the wood underneath it to protect them both from the weather. Then apply 2 coats of varnish to the inside.

A SUBTLE PLANTING
The green and gold crackle glaze on the windowbox perfectly complements this sophisticated green and golden yellow combination, with the oval-shaped leaves of the hosta contrasting with the divided fern fronds. You could position this windowbox to brighten up a sunless spot, because this combination of plants will thrive in shade.

Mimulus luteus (Monkey flower)

Polystichum setiferum Divisilobum Group

Asplenium scolopendrium Cristatum Group

Hosta ventricosa 'Aureomaculata'

The crackle effect reveals the gold paint beneath the olive green

DECORATIVE WOODEN FINISHES

You can add interest to a plain box by decorating the surface with strips of wooden molding, mitered and tacked to the front of the box (*below*) to look like paneling. Lengths of beading give a ribbed effect (*see facing page*); you could stain or paint this box in stripes of alternate colors (*see p.33*). Estimate the amount of molding or beading required before starting either project. A weatherproof preservative needs to be applied inside and out.

CREATING A SIMPLE PANELED EFFECT

YOU NEED:

MATERIALS
• Length of molding
• ¾in/20mm galvanized tacks
(Lengths and quantities required depend on the size of the windowbox)

TOOLS
• Tape measure
• Pencil
• Miter box
• Panel saw
• Hammer
• Nail punch

1 Mark out a rectangle for the molding's outer edge on the front of the box. Measure the long and the short sides, and mark out 2 of each on the outer edge of the molding.

2 Use a miter box to cut each of the 4 pieces of molding at each end, making sure that the angles slant inward from your mark to the inner edge of the molding.

3 Position the molding on the windowbox and place the tacks in a groove of the molding. Then hammer in the tacks using a nail punch to hide their heads in the groove.

FINAL FLOURISH
Paint or preservative is essential to protect the wood – and can complement flower and foliage colors.

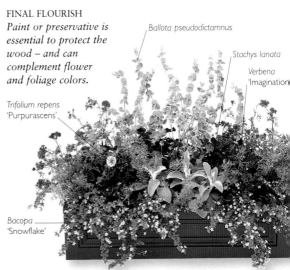

Ballota pseudodictamnus

Stachys lanata

Verbena 'Imagination'

Trifolium repens 'Purpurascens'

Bacopa 'Snowflake'

ADDING STRIPS OF BEADING

YOU NEED:

MATERIALS
• Length of ¾in/22mm half-round beading
• Length of ½×1¼in/12×32mm doorstop to use as capping
• ¾in/22mm galvanized tacks
(Lengths and quantities depend on windowbox size)

TOOLS
• Miter box
• Panel saw
• Drill and fine drill bit
• Hammer

1 Cut the beading into lengths the same depth as the windowbox, using a miter box to ensure 90° angles.

2 Drill a fine hole near each end of all the pieces to prevent splitting when tacking in place. Drill onto a scrap.

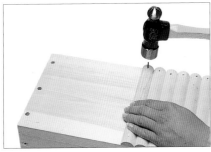

3 Lay the pieces of beading in a row along the front of the box. Adjust the spacing across the width if necessary so that the beading fits exactly, and tack it in place. Also tack 2–3 pieces at the front of each end.

4 To cut the capping, measure first from the front edge of the beading to the back of the box. When measuring the long sides, include the end beading. Cut the 4 pieces with 45° angled ends (*see Step 2, facing page*).

5 Lay the capping around the top of the box. Position all 4 pieces before tacking, since they might well need some adjusting. Secure them in place with more pins. Finish the box by applying paint or preservative.

PRACTICAL TIPS
• Since fine drill bits have a tendency to break very easily, for Step 2 you can instead nip the head off one of the galvanized tacks with nippers and use the tack in the drill as a bit.
• For a very rustic, chunky effect, you could also cover the front of a basic windowbox with log roll. This is available from garden centers in varying lengths and sizes.

PLACING WINDOWBOXES IN POSITION

Different styles of window call for different methods of attachment. You can use brackets (*see p.30*) under casement windows that open outward. The box must be secure, especially important if overlooking a sidewalk.

On sloping sills (8in/20cm front to back minimum), wedges will hold the box level; for added safety, run strong wire around the front attached to vine eyes mounted to the wall. Use a tray to catch any water that may drip.

MAKING WEDGES FOR A SLOPING SILL

YOU NEED:

MATERIALS
• Wood scrap, top 2 corners cut at right angles, 1¼in/30mm narrower than windowbox
• Wood preservative

TOOLS
• Small level
• Tape measure
• Pencil • Try square
• Vise or other clamping device
• Panel saw
• Hammer
• Long tacks

1 **To assess the slope** of the windowsill, lay a small level on the sill from the inner to the outer edge, and raise it until it is completely level.

2 **Measure and note** the gap between the level and the front of the windowsill. This gives you the measurement for the thick end of the wedge.

3 **Mark this measurement** down one side of the scrap and join with a thick line (the saw blade width) to the other corner to make the shape of the wedge.

4 **Mark out** a second identical wedge on the other side of the diagonal line, and then cut out both wedges. Treat with the same preservative as the windowbox.

5 **Using** tacks, secure the wedges onto the base of the box, at least 8in/20cm from each end.

SECURING A BOX ON A WINDOWSILL

YOU NEED:

MATERIALS
- Mirror plates
- Screws
- Hooks

TOOLS
- Tape measure
- Pencil
- Awl
- Screwdriver

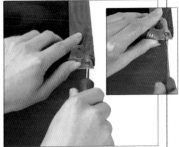

1 **Measure the width** of the window frame. Halve this measurement and mark it on the ends of the box to give the position of the center of the mirror plates.

2 **Hold the mirror plates** in place on the windowbox. Start holes with an awl to stop the wood from splitting, then screw in position (*see inset*).

4 **Screw the hooks** into the window frame, then lift the box into position on the windowsill, slotting the holes in the mirror plates over the hooks. It is usually easier to plant up the windowbox once it is in place on the sill.

3 **Rest the box** on the sill and mark the position of each hook on the window frame, using the hook itself.

PLANTING UP
Making your own windowbox means that it will fit the sill exactly and the display of plants can extend to the full width of the window. Here, pink and plum-colored pansies and ornamental cabbages have been chosen for a winter arrangement that matches the color of the box. Variegated ivy helps soften the edges.

WOODEN PLANTERS

EVEN THE SIMPLEST SQUARE WOODEN PLANTER is expensive to buy, but if you have a knack for making things – and an eye for three-dimensional jigsaw puzzles – planters really are easy to make. The two projects here require neither complicated carpentry joins nor specialized tools, and if you ask your lumber supplier to cut the wood to length it will greatly speed up the job.

MAKING A PLAIN BOX PLANTER

This planter (*left*) is constructed in layers, each one screwed to the one beneath. The layers consist of 2 long side pieces and 2 slightly shorter ones. As the layers are built up, the pieces are alternated – long over short, short over long – so that the corners overlap and the planter is held firmly together. Position screws carefully so that you do not try to put one into another below it.

YOU NEED:

MATERIALS
- 18 side pieces
18×2×2in/45×4.5×4.5cm
- 18 side pieces
14×2×2in/36×4.5×4.5cm
- 2 base slats
14×¾×¾in/36×2×2cm
- 2 base slats
12½×¾×¾in/32×2×2cm
- 2 base boards
14×5½×¾in/36×14×2cm
- 1 base board
14×3×¾in/36×7.5×2cm
- 4 pieces of capping
19×3×¾in/48×7×2cm
- 4 blocks for the feet
1¾×1¾×1¾in/4.5×4.5×4.5cm
(These measurements are for finished, planed wood.)

TOOLS
- Electric drill
- ⅛in/4mm drill bit
- ½in/13mm drill bit (for drainage holes only)
- Panel saw
- 80   3in/7.5cm screws
- 30   1¼in/3.2cm screws
- Miter box • Screwdriver
- Try square
- Pencil and tape measure
- Countersink
- Wood filler

HOW THE PARTS FIT TOGETHER

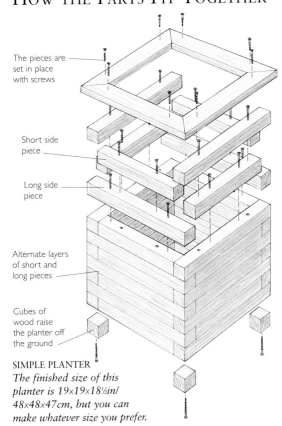

The pieces are set in place with screws

Short side piece

Long side piece

Alternate layers of short and long pieces

Cubes of wood raise the planter off the ground

SIMPLE PLANTER
The finished size of this planter is 19×19×18½in/ 48×48×47cm, but you can make whatever size you prefer.

◀ COOL SIMPLICITY *Tall stems of agapanthus and galtonia are balanced by a large planter.*

STARTING THE PLANTER

1 **Drill 4 holes,** using a ⅛in/4mm bit, in 2 long side pieces – one at each end and 2 evenly spaced in between – and 2 holes in 2 short side pieces, each a third of the way from the end.

2 **Set out 2 long and 2 short** undrilled side pieces to form a square, checking with a try square that they are at right angles. These pieces form the first layer of the planter.

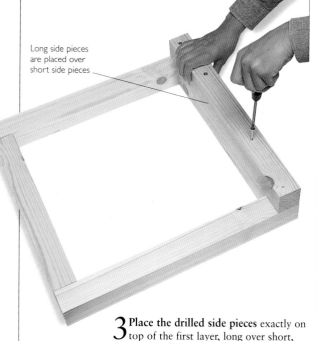

Long side pieces are placed over short side pieces

3 **Place the drilled side pieces** exactly on top of the first layer, long over short, short over long, and put in place using 3in/7.5cm screws. This is the basic method.

4 **Drill, then screw** the base slats to the inside lower edge of the first layer, using 1¼in/3.2cm screws.

BUILDING UP THE SIDES

6 **Miter the corners** on the capping at a 45° angle using a miter box. Make each piece 19in/48cm on the longer, outer edge. Drill and countersink holes on the ends and in the center.

5 **Build up the sides** by repeating step 3, first drilling holes in the side pieces and continuing to place long pieces above short and short above long until all are used. On the top layer, use only 2 screws in each piece.

7 **Screw the pieces** of capping in place using 1¼in/ 3.2cm screws. The capping should overhang the sides of the planter by ½in/1.5cm, but check that all 4 pieces make an exact fit before setting the screws.

8 **Drill holes** through the center of each of the 4 blocks to be used for the feet and screw them, using 3in/ 7.5cm screws, to each corner of the bottom of the planter.

9 **Make a couple** of drainage holes in each of the base boards using the ½in/13mm bit, then drop them into position so that they rest on the base slats. Arrange them so that the narrow one sits in the middle with the wider ones on either side. The base is designed to be removable and, if necessary, renewable. Finish by filling in the countersunk holes in the top capping with wood filler. Varnish inside and out to preserve the wood.

MAKING A CLASSIC PLANTER

This requires some forethought, so run through the steps first to make sure you understand how it fits together. Start by making two complete sides, then join these with the remaining panels

(see pp.46–47). It is essential that these first sides form a pair. To help achieve this, mark the part of the posts that faces inward and the base of each post; always work from the top.

HOW THE PIECES FIT TOGETHER

THE METHOD
There are no difficult joins. Instead, slats and screws are used to keep all the pieces together, as shown in the photographs.

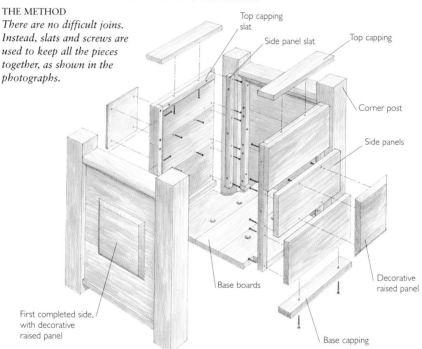

Top capping slat

Side panel slat

Top capping

Corner post

Side panels

First completed side, with decorative raised panel

Base boards

Decorative raised panel

Base capping

YOU NEED:

MATERIALS
- 4 corner posts
21½x2¾x2¾in/54.5×7×7cm
- 8 side panel slats
17x¾x¾in/43×2×2cm
- 12 side panels
12½x5¾x¾in/32×14.5×2cm
- 4 top capping slats
11x¾x¾in/28×2×2cm
- 4 pieces of top capping
12½x2¾x¾in/32×7×2cm

- 4 pieces of base capping
12½x1¾x¾in/32×4.5×2cm
- 2 base boards
15x5¾x¾in/38×14.5×2cm
- 1 base board
15x3½x¾in/38×9×2cm
- 4 decorative raised panels
7½x7½x1in/19×19×2.5cm
- 80 1¼in/3.2cm screws
- 20 2in/5cm screws

‡All measurements given here are for finished, planed wood.)

TOOLS
- Pencil
- Tape measure
- Electric drill
- ⅛in/4mm drill bit
- Screwdriver
- Try square
- ½in/13mm drill bit
- Small plane

MAKING THE FIRST SIDE

1 On each of a pair of corner posts, make a mark 2¼in/5.7cm from the top and draw a line down the center of each inside face. Shade the inner area so you always know which it is.

2 Take 4 side panel slats and drill 3 holes in each, one hole at either end and one in the center, using the ⅛in/4mm drill bit. Always drill onto a scrap of wood.

3 Screw 2 slats to each of the pair of corner posts, lining them up with the top mark and just outside your inner shaded area. Always use 1¼in/3.2cm screws unless otherwise stated. (The side panels will then be screwed to these slats – this forms the basic construction technique.)

4 Hold 3 side panels in turn against the outer edge of the slat, and mark and drill 2 holes per panel in the slat to set them in place.

5 Lay the 3 side panels in place (propped up by a scrap) and screw them to the slat. Repeat the process to attach them to the other post.

6 Drill 2 holes in a top capping slat, then screw it to the top side panel. This will be used to hold the top capping in place (*see next page*).

7 **Drill 2 holes** from top to bottom through the top capping slat (avoid the screws that attach it to the side panel) and screw it to the top capping to keep it in place.

8 **Drill 3 holes** in a piece of base capping and screw it (using 2in/5cm screws) into the bottom side panel. It is easiest if you stand the side upside down.

ADDING THE DECORATIVE DETAIL

2 **Shave off** the corner as far as each line, using a small plane.

1 **Mark lines** ½in/12mm from the corner on the top and down the side of the raised panel to show the amount to be chamfered.

3 **Mark the position** of the raised panel on the outside of this first side, making sure that it is in the center. Mark only the corners. Drill 4 holes within the marked area. (The direction of the grain should match the side panels.)

4 **Screw the panel** in place from the inside. Repeat all these stages to make 2 complete sides.

ASSEMBLING THE PLANTER

1 **Screw 3 side panels** to one corner post on each of the finished sides to form 2 right-angled halves of the planter. Join these together to complete all 4 planter walls.

2 **Having drilled and set** the remaining 2 top capping slats in place (*see p.45, Step 6*), screw the remaining 2 pieces of top capping in position (*above*).

3 **Screw the 2 pieces** of base capping in place, then the raised panels. Drop the base boards, drilled with drainage holes, into position. Paint or varnish the planter.

DUSKY TONES
The color of this planter completes a carefully thought-out design. The pale slate blue emphasizes the depth of color of the tulips and purple sage, while the acid green and flame-colored bracts of the euphorbias in the border provide a brilliant contrast. When they have finished flowering, the tulips can be replaced by a selection of annuals in equally interesting colors.

TROUGHS

WORN, WEATHERED, AND TURNING GRAY-GREEN with patches of lichen, old stone troughs make a perfect setting for plants. Their cost, though, puts them beyond the reach of most gardeners. By adapting a plastic or styrofoam crate you can make a very attractive substitute for a fraction of the price. You can even make small, substitute "rocks" from hypertufa mixture and place them among the plants, as in the arrangement opposite.

MAKING A HYPERTUFA TROUGH

The traditional alternative to stone is a ceramic sink coated with hypertufa: a mix of cement, sand, and peat. But a plastic storage crate is much cheaper and, once coated, possible to lift without the aid of a forklift. Styrofoam boxes (*see pp.52–53*) also work well. Peat substitutes can be used in the hypertufa, but bark chips do not bind, making the mix fall apart.

YOU NEED:

MATERIALS
• Plastic crate
• Chicken wire
• 12 wire ties, each about 3in/8cm long
• Cement
• Sharp sand
• Peat or peat substitute
• Water
• Natural yogurt (or liquid manure)
(Quantities of cement, sand, and peat and the length of the chicken wire will all depend on the size of the crate. Proportions are given on the next page.)

TOOLS
• Drill, preferably electric
• ½in/13mm drill bit, for making drainage holes
• Nippers or pliers
• 3-gallon/12-liter bucket or large board, for mixing hypertufa
• Trowel or spade, for mixing
• Rubber gloves
• Paintbrush

PREPARING THE CRATE

1 Make sure the crate is clean and dry. With collapsible crates (*left*), make sure they are fully open and clicked into position. Measure the height and width of each side in preparation for cutting the chicken wire covering (*see next page*).

2 Drill some evenly spaced drainage holes. You usually need 4–6 depending on the size of the crate. An electric drill at high speed is much less likely to crack the plastic than other methods. Drilling onto a scrap piece of wood protects your work surface.

◄ AMONG THE ROCKS *A pretty planting of campanulas, primroses, sedums, and saxifrages.*

COVERING WITH WIRE AND HYPERTUFA

2 Cover the crate inside and outside with the chicken wire, bending each piece firmly around the corners and tucking it securely around the base. The wire provides the "key" for the hypertufa to adhere to the crate.

1 Cut 4 pieces of chicken wire, each large enough to cover the inside and outside of one side. Allow for the pieces to overlap around the corners and tuck under the base by at least 3–4in/8–10cm.

4 Mix the hypertufa using, by volume, 1 part cement, 1 part sharp sand, and 1–2 parts dry peat or peat substitute. Combine the dry ingredients thoroughly, then add sufficient water to make a stiff mortar. Avoid making the mix too wet, or it will not adhere.

PRACTICAL TIPS

• Stand the crate on bricks while applying the hypertufa.
• Allow the hypertufa to set naturally – the slower the better. You can, if you want, cover it with plastic or damp burlap.
• Avoid working with hypertufa in cold weather.

3 Thread the wire ties from the outside to the inside of the crate, then back through to tie together the two layers of chicken wire. Use 2–4 ties on each side. This helps prevent a cavity from forming in the hypertufa when it is applied both inside and outside the crate.

5 **Press the hypertufa** in handfuls against the crate walls, inside and out and just under (but not covering) the base. Push it through the chicken wire so that the two layers bond to form a solid wall. Smooth the surface as you go to prevent cracks.

6 **Allow to harden** and, once the hypertufa is dry (usually 2–3 days), paint the surface with yogurt (or liquid manure) to encourage the growth of algae. This helps give the trough a much more natural look.

MAKING HYPERTUFA ROCKS

Rocks can greatly enhance alpines in a trough, but, to help save natural limestone deposits and similar areas from unnecessary quarrying, why not try making hypertufa rocks? It is almost inevitable that there will be some mix left over. Simply put some in a plastic bag (*see right*) and shape it into a rock (it may help to have a photograph to copy). Allow to dry slowly. Before the rock hardens completely, you can refine its appearance by adding a few crevices and naturalistic marks.

CHOOSING APPROPRIATE PLANTS
The plants you choose depend on the size of trough and where you plan to put it. These lavenders suit a large container destined for a sunny spot. Rock garden plants (see pp.76–77) are the classic choice. They often have small roots and will do well in shallow troughs.

FAKING A ROCK

TEXTURED CEMENT TROUGH

A styrofoam crate encased in cement mixed with reinforcing fibers produces a trough that is strong, light, and has good insulating qualities. You may need to search around for the best source of the crate; reinforcing fibers are used in building ponds and pools and may be found in aquatic plant nurseries. It is not necessary to paint the trough, but a subtle bit of color can make a welcome change from the natural stone look.

YOU NEED:

MATERIALS
- Styrofoam crate
- PVA adhesive
- Cement
- Sharp sand
- Reinforcing fibers
- Water
- Masonry paint

TOOLS
- Drill or knife
- 4–6 corks
- Bricks to stand the crate on
- Large bucket or board, for mixing
- Rubber gloves

MAKING THE TROUGH

1 **Make some** drainage holes in the crate base with a knife or drill and plug with corks so that each cork juts out an inch beyond the outside of the crate. (The corks will be removed once the cement has set.)

2 **Turn the crate** upside down, keeping it off the ground with a stack of bricks, and coat the outside with a thick layer of PVA adhesive. Leave until the adhesive turns tacky, while you make the cement mixture.

3 **Mix the cement coating** by combining 2 parts cement with 1 part sand, by volume, then adding a handful of the fibers. Fluff them out and work them through the mixture, then add enough water to make a stiff mortar.

4 **Press small handfuls** of the mixture all over the outside of the crate, smoothing the surface as you go. The coating needs to be only a half inch thick. When it has hardened a little, turn the crate the right way up.

6 **Paint the trough,** if desired, once the cement has completely hardened, with masonry or other suitable exterior-quality paint. Remove the corks to create the drainage holes.

PRACTICAL HINTS

• If you prefer, you can give the trough a smooth finish by burning off the ends of the fibers before painting.

• Because this type of reinforcing fiber makes the cement mixture exceptionally strong, the coating around the crate can be made quite thin (just over ½in/1cm) without any danger of the trough cracking.

• If using a crate once holding foodstuffs, after rinsing it you will probably need to allow time for the odor to disappear.

5 **Cover the bucket** of cement mix with a damp cloth. Paint the rim and inner edge with PVA, and wait for it to go tacky. Press more mixture around the crate top and down the inside walls to just below planting level.

CHOOSING PLANTS

Rock garden plants such as small campanulas, achilleas, and sedums are ideal for shallow troughs. The diascia is not reliably hardy and will need to be renewed the following season. For this kind of planting, it is essential to use a free-draining soil mix (see p.55).

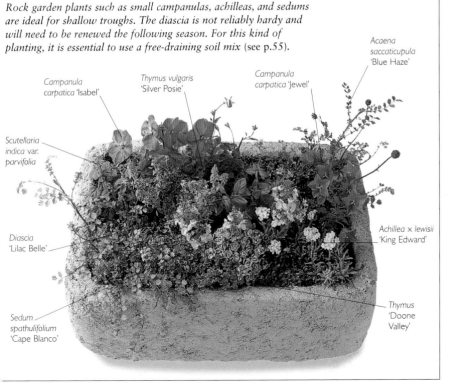

Acaena saccaticupula 'Blue Haze'

Campanula carpatica 'Isabel'

Thymus vulgaris 'Silver Posie'

Campanula carpatica 'Jewel'

Scutellaria indica var. *parvifolia*

Diascia 'Lilac Belle'

Sedum spathulifolium 'Cape Blanco'

Achillea × *lewisii* 'King Edward'

Thymus 'Doone Valley'

PLANTING AND ROUTINE CARE

CARING FOR PLANTS IN POTS

UNLIKE PLANTS IN THE OPEN GROUND, container plants are very dependent on watering and feeding. Evergreens may need watering even in winter, when the drying effect of wind can be particularly damaging. Regular watering tends to compact soil, so always use one of the special potting mixes available (*see opposite*), which drain freely and hold sufficient air, moisture, and nutrients to sustain plant growth. Stand containers on wedges or feet to aid drainage.

PREPARING FOR PLANTING

Make sure that there are adequate drainage holes in the base of containers; if using an improvised or homemade container, you may need to drill some. It is essential that plant roots never become waterlogged. Cover the pot base with a piece of window screening to prevent loss of soil mix without impeding drainage. It is also a good idea to use pot feet or wedges to raise the container slightly so that water can drain freely, especially in winter. As a precaution against the soil mix drying out for short periods, mix in water-retentive crystals, which swell up with moisture then later release it. When planting in large containers, more surface area of the soil mix is exposed to sunlight, so it is a good idea to mulch with pebbles or gravel to conserve moisture.

GRAVEL

STYROFOAM

Crystals swell on contact with water

ADDING CROCKS
Broken pieces of terracotta, or "crocks," are the most traditional material for covering the base of a container, but gravel, styrofoam pieces, or a piece of screen are good alternatives.

USING WATER-RETENTIVE CRYSTALS
Mix water-retentive crystals thoroughly into the soil mix before planting to help plants through short dry spells. Never add more than the recommended amount.

WHICH SOIL MIX TO CHOOSE

Do not be tempted to use garden soil for container planting, because of the danger of introducing pests, worms, weed seeds, and even diseases. Using a formulated potting mix eliminates all these risks. Chosen carefully for the particular planting you have in mind (for instance, there are mixes designed specially for trees and shrubs), it will include exactly the right balance of nutrients and adequate drainage material to encourage healthy plant growth over a period of time. Soil-based mixes contain prepared, sterilized soil of ideal texture and composition and are heavy, often making pots more stable. Peat- or peat substitute-based mixes are light but, if they dry out, can be difficult to moisten again.

A great advantage of container growing is that you can provide for the likes and dislikes of particular plants. Favorite plants that do not grow well in your garden's soil can be encouraged to thrive in containers filled with a soil mix tailor-made to meet their requirements.

TYPES OF SOIL MIX

SOIL-BASED

Soil-based mixes vary from supplier to supplier, so buy a sample bag before buying a large quantity. These mixes are all quite heavy when wet, but they hold nutrients for a considerable time. They are suitable for trees and shrubs, such as *Fatsia japonica* (*right*), and also for perennials.

GENERAL-PURPOSE (SOILLESS)

Peat- or peat substitute-based multipurpose mixes are ideal for flowering annuals, such as *Tagetes* (*right*), and plants that are used in displays that last for only a few months. These mixes are light and easy to handle but dry out easily and need regular checking.

ACIDIC

Plants that cannot tolerate lime, such as azaleas, rhododendrons, and pieris, need acidic, or "ericaceous," compost. Lime also affects flower color in plants such as hydrangeas (*right*). Use an acidic mix if blue-flowered cultivars are to stay blue.

ALPINE (FREE-DRAINING)

Alpine soil mix includes plenty of coarse grit to give the extra drainage needed by rock garden plants, such as *Androsace* (*right*). You can also mix your own by adding grit to a soil-based mix. A surface dressing of coarse grit helps prevent stem rot due to winter moisture.

PLANTING IN CONTAINERS

SMALL TREES, SHRUBS, AND PERENNIALS that will live in containers long-term need a soil mix that will satisfy their nutritional demands over an extended period. They also require good-sized containers, large enough for their roots to develop properly and heavy enough to stay upright in wind. Annuals and small bulbs are useful for adding seasonal color under permanent plantings.

PLANTING INDIVIDUAL SHRUBS

When planting a single specimen shrub for immediate impact, it is best to choose a plant that is 2–3 years old and container-grown in a large pot. The new container must be sturdy and large enough to allow a minimum of 2–3in/5–8cm of new soil mix under the shrub's root ball and around its sides. If the pot has no drainage hole, there must also be sufficient depth for a layer of drainage material to be added. Before planting, it is important to water the shrub thoroughly and allow it to drain.

1 **Fill the container** loosely with some soil mix. Use the shrub's old pot as a guide to check that the plant will sit at the correct depth.

2 **Tease out** some fine roots gently around the sides and base of the root ball. Lower the shrub into the container. Firm the plant in.

3 **Add any extra** soil mix that is needed, making sure you leave space at the top of the pot for watering. Water in thoroughly.

UNDERPLANTING A SHRUB

Some fast-growing shrubs (like the pieris, right) require large containers such as half-barrels to accommodate their roots and provide a visual balance to their ultimate size. To give the planting additional interest while the shrub is small, use colorful annuals, which, with their shallow roots, will not compete for food or space. Late winter-flowering pansies make an excellent choice for a site that catches the sun at that time of year. They will be happy in the acidic soil mix used for the pieris. In summer, there is a wider range of bedding plants to choose from.

The barrel must be waterproofed inside and out

Barrel must have drainage holes

Making the Most of Bulbs

Many bulbs, such as daffodils, are resilient enough to be planted in up to 3 layers in a large pot. Concentrating a number of bulbs in a small area gives a generous display. Ivy will cascade over the edges of the pot, and pansies will produce a second flush just as daffodils come into bloom.

Dense planting of daffodils provides masses of flowers

Pansies require some sun to bloom

Ivy planted at edge

Bulbs are planted in alternate tiers

1 **Cross-section** shows a drainage layer, 3 layers of bulbs in general-purpose soil mix, and surface planting.

2 **Interest is** maintained by variegated ivy and pansies. Deadheading encourages new blooms.

3 **In spring** the display is at its best, with the daffodils blooming above a carpet of ivy and pansies.

Mixed Plantings

Spring-planted perennials will make splendid container displays through summer, but you may need to divide and replant them for the following season, particularly if grouping more than one plant in a pot. Site the tallest plants in the center of the display, and let trailing types spill over the edges.

Heuchera micrantha 'Palace Purple'

Penstemon 'Rich Ruby'

Artemisia 'Powis Castle'

Geranium sanguineum var. *striatum*

◄ PLANTING TIME
Group the plants while still in their pots to decide on the best arrangement. Then plant, firm in, and water well.

▶ IN FULL GLORY
This display uses plants with good contrasts in foliage color and forms. Most perennials tolerate trimming if they start swamping their neighbors.

ROUTINE CARE

PLANTS IN CONTAINERS NEED REGULAR ATTENTION. Do not rely on rainfall to keep them watered. The soil mix needs to be kept appropriately moist. Use pot feet or wedges to raise containers off the ground and allow water to drain freely. Fast-acting liquid fertilizers are easy to use. Choose those high in nitrogen for foliage plants and high-potassium formulations for flowers.

WATERING AND FEEDING

In summer try to water at the start or end of the day, when less will be lost through evaporation. Hot sun on wet leaves may cause spotting. A slow-release fertilizer plug pushed into soil mix supplies nutrients gradually, but for maximum flowers give plants a biweekly boost of tomato fertilizer.

SLOW-RELEASE FERTILIZER PLUGS

Direct the water to the soil mix; if sprinkled onto leaves it will run straight off

EFFECTIVE WATERING
Soak the soil mix directly or fill a saucer or tray beneath so that the plant takes it up.

RENEWING THE DISPLAY

Remove bedding plants from containers when they finish flowering, disturbing those that remain as little as possible. To maintain the display, replace them with plants that have a later flowering season or striking foliage. You can also add bulbs to continue interest over a longer period.

DEADHEADING
Deadheading is vital to encourage plants to continue flowering. Pinch off dead blooms between your thumb and forefinger.

Pick off any dead leaves regularly

Evergreen foliage plants such as ivy give year-round interest

1 **Remove plants** that have finished flowering, taking care not to damage the roots of remaining plants. Continue deadheading to encourage more flowers.

2 **Add fresh potting mix** and fill the gaps with new plants or bulbs that will continue the display. Firm gently and water thoroughly to help the new plants establish.

REPLENISHING SOIL MIX

Most shrubs, once fully grown, can stay in the same pot for several years if nourished by a top-dressing of fresh potting mix applied each spring. To ensure good plant growth, combine fertilizer with the soil mix.

Soil mix loses its nutrients in time

TOP-DRESSING
Scrape off about 2in/5cm of soil mix. Replace this top layer with fresh mix combined with a slow-release fertilizer. Water thoroughly.

WINTER SHELTER

Many container plants will not survive winter cold. Any with foliage that dies down can be put in a barely heated shed or garage. Others need protection and light.

• Even normally hardy plants are vulnerable in pots. In many areas, or if a plant is described as "borderline hardy," move to the most sheltered side of the house or bury to the rim in a border and mulch with dry straw.

• Marginally hardy plants need to be moved into a cold frame or greenhouse. Some survive outside if pots are wrapped in burlap or bubble wrap to insulate roots. Use this to wrap leaves, too, of phormiums and yuccas.

• Marginally hardy plants can also be put in a barely heated sunroom or conservatory.

• Tender plants (e.g. citrus) need to be moved into a heated greenhouse or conservatory.

Protect your back – use a trolley or board fitted with casters to move large containers.

REPOTTING AN OVERGROWN PLANT

When a plant outgrows its container, it will lose vigor and start showing signs of poor health, such as yellowing leaves. To check whether it needs repotting, remove the plant carefully from its container and examine the roots. If they are crowded, you need to repot the plant into a larger container. Select one that is one or two sizes larger. Make sure that it is clean in order to avoid introducing diseases.

1 Ease the plant gently from its pot by a combination of tapping the rim and pulling gently on the base of the stems.

2 Tease out roots that have become very congested, and cut back thick roots by about a third. Leave the thin fibrous roots intact.

3 Put fresh soil mix in the new pot and lower in the plant. Add soil mix around the edges and firm in. Add support for climbers (*here ivy*) and tie in stems (*see inset*). Water well.

TRAINING STANDARDS

STANDARD PLANTS IN POTS can bring formal elegance to courtyards, patios, and doorways. Standards that are destined for a prominent position deserve a handsome but sturdy container. Choose a size and style that will balance the height and width of the plant. When fully grown, most standards need regular trimming to keep them in shape and frequent feeding in the growing season.

TRAINING A STANDARD FUCHSIA

Shrubby plants such as fuchsias grow quickly and produce soft shoots that can be "pinch-pruned" to make bushy heads. No equipment is needed; sideshoots and then shoot tips, once the head starts to form, are pinched out between finger and thumb. Start with a young plant about 6in/15cm high. Generally, it takes 6 months to achieve an 18in/45cm standard and 18 months to grow a full 3ft/1m-high standard, so, where not hardy, plants will need shelter in winter.

OTHER SUITABLE PLANTS

Argyranthemum frutescens
Cascade chrysanthemums
Helichrysum petiolare
Heliotropium arborescens (Heliotrope)
Lantana camara
Solenostemon scutellaroides (Coleus)

FLOWERS GALORE
Choose a vigorous, free-flowering fuchsia. Remove old leaves from the main stem that do not naturally fall.

1 **Pinch out** any sideshoots as they appear in the leaf angles. Insert a stake and tie in the stem to keep it straight.

2 **Keep removing** sideshoots (never the tip) to produce a tall, straight stem. Transfer to a bigger pot with a taller stake.

3 **When the stem** is 3 sets of leaves taller than you want the clear trunk of the standard to be, pinch out the growing tip.

4 **Pinch out** the tips of the sideshoots at the top of the stem to make them branch further. Repeat until a round head is formed.

TRAINING STANDARD TREES

Many trees, such as citrus and bays, can be bought as standards but are expensive. If you have a little patience, they are not particularly difficult to train yourself, though it takes several years. Start with a healthy young plant with an upright main stem that will naturally lend itself to training. Tie this in to a stake just taller than you want the clear trunk to be. You will need pruners when stems turn woody.

TREES AND SHRUBS FOR STANDARDS

Brugmansia (Angels' trumpets)
Citrus trees: Calamondin
(× *Citrofortunella microcarpa*),
a tangerine-kumquat hybrid;
Citrus × *meyeri* 'Meyer'
Laurus nobilis (Bay)

Pittosporum
Myrtus communis
Nerium oleander
Syringa meyeri
Viburnum tinus

Prune the main stem back to a strong bud just below the top of the stake

Prune shoots by 3–5 leaves. As more shoots develop, continue pruning in the same way to form a well-shaped head

Stake enables stem to grow straight

Leaves on shortened sideshoots feed and thicken the trunk

Select 4 strong, well-spaced framework shoots from which to develop the head

Remove all subsequent shoots from the main stem. Leaves on it will be shed naturally

Keep tip-pruning new shoots to make the head bushier

Calamondin enjoys an acidic soil mix

1 **Tie in** the main stem; tip-prune it once it reaches the desired height. Shorten side-shoots by a third in their first year; remove the year after.

2 **Let 4 strong shoots** develop to form the head. Shorten them to make them branch, then shorten their sideshoots in turn.

A MATURE TREE
The stake and ties may be removed as soon as the stem becomes woody and the plant is well established.

CREATING INTERESTING SHAPES

SMALL-LEAVED IVIES ARE EASILY TURNED into topiary using a wire shape or, with time, you can make a masterpiece in boxwood or yew using more traditional techniques. Some plants can be pinch-pruned, enabling you to create pillars and cones, even fans, around a simple frame of stakes. Climbers can be trained over tripods, wire obelisks, or other shapes.

TRAINED AND CLIPPED TOPIARY

Some of the simplest but most effective topiary is created by letting ivy grow around a wire frame. Shoots will need occasional tying in or trimming off. You can buy specially made animal or geometric wire shapes or make your own. Try molding chicken wire into three-dimensional creatures (*see p.13*). Use a frame, too, for conventional topiary in boxwood or yew. It makes clipping much easier.

▶ IVY SEA HORSE
Plastic-coated wire has been bent into a sea horse shape. Wire zig-zagged across the center of the shape strengthens it and gives extra support for the ivy to cling to.

PLANTS FOR TOPIARY

Buxus sempervirens 'Suffruticosa' Boxwood
Ficus pumila
Hedera helix 'Needlepoint' Ivy with tiny leaves
Hedera helix 'Goldheart' Gold-variegated ivy
Taxus Yew

USING A TOPIARY FRAME

1 **Place the frame** over the plant (*here yew*), securing it into the soil. Trim the tips of all the shoots to encourage the plant to make bushy growth that will fill out the frame.

2 **Trim shoots** when they start growing beyond the edge of the frame, using the frame as a guide for cutting. Pruners are often better than shears for clipping small, detailed shapes.

3 **Foliage hides** the frame when the topiary is mature. It will need regular trimming to keep a neat outline, generally at least 3–4 times a year depending on the intricacy of the shape.

TRAINING A HELICHRYSUM CONE

With frequent pinch-pruning (*see p.60*), spreading plants such as *Helichrysum petiolare* can be trained to make a dense, leafy cone, ideal for adding height to a display. Helichrysums grow fast and should reach the top of a yard-high stake tepee in one season. In cold areas, protect under glass in winter for the following season.

Pinch sideshoots to a leaf or bud so that none extends beyond the width of the pot

Use soft twine to tie the leading, upright stems to the stakes that will form the tepee

FLORAL EFFECT

A helichrysum is grown for foliage effect but, with plants such as fuchsias and ivy-leaved geraniums, once you stop pinch-pruning, flowerbuds will form and the cone will be covered with flowers.

1 Plant 3 young plants in a pot. Insert 3 stakes, the height of the cone. Tie in the leading, upright shoots. Pinch all sideshoots to a bud or leaf in line with the edge of the pot.

Pinch the sideshoots once a week to develop a conical shape and make the plants bushy (this side still needs to be pinched)

Pinch out the tips of the leading stems once they reach the top

Pinch to keep a smooth line up the side of the cone

2 Tie the stakes to form a tepee. Keep tying in the leading shoots and pinching sideshoots to develop a dense, well-shaped cone. Put into a sturdy container for display.

FINISHED CONE
This cone has been left to grow out to give an informal look, but it could also be trimmed with shears to create a clean-cut topiary effect.

GOOD PLANTS FOR CONTAINERS

This selection of plants is arranged according to the type of container and style of display that suits them best, but there are no hard and fast rules, and planting arrangements will always need to satisfy your individual requirements.

■ *Prefers full sun* ■ *Prefers partial shade* ■ *Tolerates full shade* **CH** *Approximate height in container* **CS** *Approximate spread in container* **Z** *Hardiness zone ranges are given as Zx–x*

RECOMMENDED LARGE PLANTS

MANY OF THE FOLLOWING TREES, shrubs, and climbers make good specimen plants for large containers. Pots must be stable, and soil mix will need revitalizing regularly. Some of the most useful architectural plants are not very hardy (if at all), so in cold areas they will require winter protection (*see p.59*).

Abutilon pictum 'Thomsonii'
Shrub with orange bell flowers in summer and mottled maple-shaped leaves. Requires a sheltered sunny site; protect in winter in a greenhouse or conservatory. The abutilon 'Souvenir de Bonn' has cream-margined leaves.
■ CH 4–6½ft/1.2–2m CS 3ft/1m **Z8–10**

Acer palmatum
(Japanese maple)
Small tree good for adding a Japanese flavor. Deciduous, deeply cut leaves often show brilliant autumn color.
A. palmatum 'Dissectum Atropurpureum' (*see p.17*) has delicate, feathery leaves; avoid exposed, windy sites.
■ CH 4ft/1.2m CS 5–6½ft/1.5–2m **Z6–8**

Aralia elata
Architectural tree for light shade. Deciduous, divided leaves arranged in tiers; cream-edged leaves in 'Variegata'.
■ CH 10ft/3m CS 6½ft/2m **Z4–9**

BRUGMANSIA AUREA

Brugmansia
(Angels' trumpets, Datura)
Huge trumpets, often fragrant. Those of *B. aurea* smell best in evening. Other species can have white or pink trumpets. Flowers produced most freely within the restriction of a container. Evergreen, but needs some warmth in winter. Toxic.
■ CH 6½ft/2m CS 3–6½ft/1–2m Min 45°F/7°C

Buxus sempervirens
(Boxwood)
Ideal for container topiary (*see pp.13, 62*). Slow-growing shrub with dense stems of small evergreen leaves that can be clipped to geometric shapes. You can buy wire frames that act as a guide for clipping.
■ CH to 8ft/2.5m CS to 3ft/1m **Z6–8**

CONVOLVULUS CNEORUM

Camellia japonica
Good shrub in a container against a west or sheltered north wall where early spring flowers are less likely to be browned by frost. Many good cultivars with single or double flowers in red, pink, or white. Use acidic soil mix. ▨▨ CH 6½ft/2m CS 3ft/1m **Z7–8**

Citrus
Highly decorative and, in a warm climate, productive small trees or shrubs. Sweet-smelling white flowers are followed by fruit. *C. × meyeri* 'Meyer' is a compact hybrid lemon. × *Citrofortunella microcarpa,* the calamondin, has small decorative fruit that can be crystallized. In cold areas, must be wintered in a conservatory or greenhouse. ▨ CH to 6½ft/2m CS to 5ft/1.5m Min 37–40°F/3–5°C

Convolvulus cneorum
Sun-loving shrub with silvery leaves and white flowers that will tumble over the sides of a pot from late spring to mid-summer. Appreciates protection from wind and requires good drainage.

It can be tricky to grow. ▨ CH 18in/45cm CS 2ft/60cm **Z8–10**

Cordyline australis
Palmlike tree that creates a highly sculptural effect (*see p.10*). Some cultivars have striped or plum-colored leaves. Excellent in urban settings. Tolerates light shade but needs winter protection of a greenhouse or conservatory. ▨ CH 6½–10ft/2–3m CS 3–4ft/1–1.2m **Z10–11**

Cupressus torulosa 'Cashmeriana'
Extremely elegant conifer with sprays of pendulous blue leaves. A large tree when planted in the ground, but a container keeps it to a manageable size. Move into a greenhouse or conservatory in cold areas in winter. ▨ CH 10ft/3m CS 5ft/1.5m **Z6–9**

Cycas revoluta
Architectural, exotic-looking palmlike plant with shaggy trunk and shuttlecock of fringed leathery leaves. Native of Japan; in cold areas it needs winter warmth in a

× FATSHEDERA LIZEI

FATSIA JAPONICA

greenhouse or conservatory. ▨ CH 3–6½ft/1–2m CS 3–6½ft/1–2m Min 45–50°F/7–10°C

Eriobotrya japonica (Loquat)
Striking evergreen shrub or small tree with large, veined, leathery leaves. In a sheltered site, fragrant white autumn flowers are followed in spring by orange edible fruit. Can be grown against a sheltered sunny wall. ▨ CH 6½–10ft/2–3m CS 6½–10ft/2–3m **Z8–10**

× Fatshedera lizei
Evergreen shrub useful for training up a vertical support. Large ivylike leaves, and greenish white flowers in autumn. Particularly tolerant of poor conditions such as exposure, pollution, shade. ▨▨ CH to 6½ft/2m CS 3ft/1m **Z8–10**

Fatsia japonica
Spreading, architectural shrub for a shaded, sheltered courtyard. Evergreen, with large, glossy leaves. Creamy white autumn flowers are followed by black berries. ▨ CH 5ft/1.5m CS 3–4ft/1–1.2m **Z8–10**

Hydrangea macrophylla 'Blue Wave'

Hydrangea macrophylla
Hydrangeas look particularly good in half-barrels or wooden planters. Blue flowers are normally produced only in acidic soil, so using acidic soil mix in pots enables you to grow blue cultivars in alkaline areas. Those known as "lacecaps," such as 'Blue Wave' (*above*), have flowerheads composed of sterile and fertile flowers. The "mopheads" have rounded heads of only sterile flowers. Prune established plants in spring, cutting back one in four old flowering stems to the base. Trim off other old flower-heads to the next leaf bud. ◩ ◪ CH 3ft/1m CS 6ft/1.8m **Z6–9**

Ilex crenata (Japanese holly)
Neat holly with glossy, oval, dark green leaves. Sometimes produces white or yellow fruit from inconspicuous flowers. Makes a useful year-round shrub. 'Convexa' is broader and denser in habit and produces masses of shiny black fruits. ◩ CH 6½ft/2m CS 3ft/1m **Z5–7**

Lantana
Evergreen shrub grown for its vivid flowers, sometimes bicolored, ranging from white to yellow and salmon-pink to red or purple, in summer and autumn. Needs warmth in winter. Can be grown as a standard (*see p.60*). ◩ CH 3ft/1m CS 3ft/1m Min 50°F/10°C

Laurus nobilis (Bay)
Handsome evergreen shrub or small tree that doubles as a culinary herb. In spring, clusters of greenish yellow flowers are produced, followed by black berries on female plants only. It enjoys the warmth of a sunny wall. Adapts well to clipping and can be grown as a stanzdard (*see pp.22, 61*). ◩ CH 6½–10ft/ 2–3m CS 3–6½ft/ 1–2m **Z8–10**

Lavandula (Lavender)
Aromatic, easy to grow, and attracts butterflies and bees. *L. angustifolia* can have pink or white flowers as well as the more usual blue-purple. 'Hidcote' is compact with dense purple flower spikes. *L. stoechas* (*see p.9*) is more tender. All need free-draining soil mix. Keep lavenders in shape by cutting back in spring, always leaving some green growth. ◩ CH 2ft/60cm CS 3ft/1m **Z5–8**

Lantana 'Tangerine'

Myrtus communis

Myrtus communis
(Common myrtle)
Small aromatic shrub that will scent a sitting area. Delightful fragrant ivory flowers stand out against evergreen leaves in late summer. Take indoors in winter in most areas. *M. communis* subsp. *tarentina* has smaller leaves and makes a more rounded shape. ◩ CH 3ft/1m CS 3ft/1m **Z8–9**

Nerium oleander (Oleander)
A Mediterranean reminder for city gardens. In summer, clusters of pink, red, or white flowers cover this narrow-leaved shrub or small tree (*see p.61*). In cold areas, protect in a conservatory or greenhouse in winter. Toxic. ◩ CH 6½ft/2m CS 3–5ft/ 1–1.5m Min 36–41°F/2–5°C

Phormium tenax
(New Zealand flax)
Striking foliage plant with upright swordlike leaves. Tall stems bear heads of dull red flowers in summer. Some phormiums have bronze or interestingly striped foliage. 'Dazzler' is small with bronze leaves streaked with red,

orange, and pink; those of 'Variegatum' have creamy yellow margins. Move to a sheltered spot for winter in cold areas and insulate the container with a layer of bubblewrap or burlap. You can also wrap the leaves in a sheath of protective material.
❑ CH to 6½ft/2m
CS to 3ft/1m **Z9–10**

Rosa (Rose)
Choose dwarf cluster-flowered or miniature bush forms for growing in containers, and allow plenty of depth for their long roots. 'The Fairy' covers itself with medium pink blooms. 'Marie Pavie' bears pale pink flowers. 'Margo Koster' produces bright orange, cupped blooms. All bloom freely through summer.
❑ CH to 18in/45cm
CS to 18in/45cm **Z5–9**

Rosmarinus officinalis (Rosemary)
Aromatic shrub for a sunny site. Ideally, put in a sheltered spot near the kitchen door or barbecue – needlelike leaves are excellent for flavoring grilled food. Blue flowers cover the stems from spring to early summer. 'Prostratus' looks good trailing over the sides of a container but is more tender. Plants must have free-draining soil mix, and they benefit from winter protection. ❑ CH to 3ft/1m CS 3ft/1m **Z8–10**

Salix caprea 'Kilmarnock' (Kilmarnock willow)
Small weeping tree (*see p.16*) whose shape gives all-year interest. Bare branches in spring are studded with furry catkins. A subtly colored planter and ring of crocuses can complete the picture.
❑ CH 5–6½ft/1.5–2m
CS 6½ft/2m **Z6–8**

Viburnum tinus (Laurustinus)
A shade-tolerant and reliable shrub for a container; it can also be grown as a standard (*see p.61*). The flat heads of white flowers against evergreen leaves look good in winter. Underplant with annual bedding for summer color.
❑❑❑ CH 4ft/1.2m CS 4ft/1.2m **Z8–10**

Yucca
Spiky evergreen for a sunny corner (*see p.27*). Match its exotic looks with a handsome container. Tall spikes of white bells rise from the center in summer. *Y. filamentosa* is quite small and is hardy in Zones 5–10. *Y. gloriosa* and yellow-striped 'Variegata' are tall and hardy in Zones 7–10. Can be protected in the same way as a phormium (*see left*). Use free-draining soil mix.
❑ CH to 5ft/1.5m CS to 3ft/1m Hardiness varies

SOME CLIMBERS FOR CONTAINERS

These climbers give color and height. For support, insert a tepee of stakes or use one of the attractive specially made frames, a trellis, or willow branch.

Ipomoea tricolor **'Heavenly Blue'** (Morning glory)
Succession of glorious azure trumpets open each morning in a sunny spot. Fast-growing; grow as an annual. Start from seed on an indoor windowsill. Put several plants in one large pot.
❑ CH 10ft/3m Annual

Lathyrus odoratus (Sweet pea)
Provides delicious scent in summer and early autumn. Huge range of colors available; regular picking prolongs flowering. An annual, but you may find pots of seedlings or raise your own from seed. The Bijou Group is smaller, needing less support, but has less scent.
❑ CH to 6½ft/2m Annual

Plumbago auriculata
Evergreen climbing shrub with sky blue flowers from summer to late autumn as long as roots are not kept too wet. It needs protection in winter in most areas. Good in conservatories. ❑ CH 10ft/3m CS 3–10ft/1–3m **Z9–10**

LATHYRUS 'NOEL SUTTON'

PLANTS FOR GROUPED CONTAINERS

SOME OF THE MOST EFFECTIVE displays combine separate pots, each containing a different type of plant. Individual needs, such as special soil mix or winter protection, can be provided for and plants easily added or removed without disturbing roots. The following work well in this kind of arrangement.

FUCHSIA 'LADY THUMB'

Agapanthus
Round heads of blue or white flowers on tall stems in mid–late summer (*see p.40*). Plants can be moved into position when about to flower. A few are fairly hardy, but in most areas put into a shed or cold frame for winter or sink pot into the ground. ◘ CH to 3ft/1m CS to 2ft/60cm **Z7–10**

Chrysanthemum
Rubellum chrysanthemums make good late summer and early autumn pot plants, in a variety of colors with yellow centers to the flowers. They form bushy plants with slightly silvery foliage. ◘ CH 2ft/60cm CS to 2ft/60cm **Z6–9**

Eucomis bicolor
Striking spikes of green flowers in late summer (*see p.19*). A bulbous perennial that needs

to be overwintered indoors in many areas. ◘ CH to 2ft/60cm CS to 12in/30cm **Z8–10**

Fuchsia
Upright fuchsias add height when grown as standards (*see p.60*). Trailing types are ideal for a tall pot or windowbox (*see p.30*). Wide choice, with single or double flowers in combinations of red, white, pink, and purple, produced all summer. Most need minimally heated winter protection. Plantlets available in spring. ◘ CH to 2ft/60cm (as a bush) CS to 2ft/60cm **Z8–10**

Galtonia candicans
Summer bulb with white tubular flowers (*see p.40*). Protect pots or lift bulbs for winter in cold climates. ◘ CH 3–4ft/1–1.2m CS 12in/10cm **Z7–10**

Helianthus annuus
Sunflowers (*see p.7*) in pots can be moved around so that they face you, not the sun. Choose short-growing types such as 'Music Box' with flowers from creamy yellow to dark red. Annual; easy to raise from seed. ◘ CH 18in/45cm CS 18in/45cm Annual

Lilium (Lily)
Lilies give color, many have wonderful fragrance, and, grown in their own pot, can be moved at their peak into prime position. Use deep pots and plant bulbs at 2–3 times their depth. The majority prefer acidic soil mix, but check individual species and hybrids. Short-growing lilies are easier than tall types, which need staking. Feed occasionally with high-potassium fertilizer. There is a

INTERESTING SUCCULENTS

With their rosettes of fleshy leaves, succulents have an interesting textural quality, especially if planted in a terracotta pot. They need gritty, free-draining soil mix.

Aeonium arboreum
One of the taller succulents. The leaves of 'Zwartkop' are almost black (*see p.8*). Perennial, but overwinter in

a conservatory or heated greenhouse.
◘ CH 2ft/60cm CS 3ft/1m Min 50°F/7°C

Echeveria elegans
Rosettes of silver-blue leaves are sometimes edged red. Best grown as an annual. Useful for shallow pots.
◘ CH 2in/5cm CS 20in/50cm Min 45°F/7°C

LILIUM 'STAR GAZER'

huge range to choose from, for sun or part shade. For midsummer fragrance, try white *L. regale*; it varies in height. The following Asiatic hybrids lack scent but are easy to grow: 'Connecticut King', with rich yellow, long-lasting flowers; 'Enchantment', orange and short-growing; scarlet 'Fire King'; 'Mont Blanc', short-growing with bowl-shaped white flowers. Pinkish red, unscented 'Star Gazer' also flowers at this time; it is quite tall. Later in summer come *L. auratum* with white flowers banded gold and tall *L. speciosum* with white flowers spotted crimson; both are fragrant but more tricky. ◨◧ CH to 4ft/1.2m CS 8in/20cm **Z5–8**

Tulipa (Tulip)
Extensive range for spring flowers (*see pp.11, 19*). Some short-stemmed types, such as scarlet 'Fusilier' and pink and cream 'Heart's Delight', are good for windowsills. After foliage dies down, lift and replant bulbs in garden.
◨ CH to 2ft/60cm CS 4in/10cm **Z4–7**

GOOD FOLIAGE PLANTS

Asplenium scolopendrium
(Hart's tongue fern)
Glossy evergreen fronds brighten a shady corner. Some kinds have crested, wavy-edged fronds.
◨◧ CH 18–28in/45–70cm CS 2ft/60cm **Z6–8**

Chionochloa conspicua
(Plumed tussock grass)
Ornamental grass with tussocks of red-brown leaves that bear elegant plumes of creamy flowerheads in mid–late summer. Makes an excellent container specimen in 2–3 years. Protect from winter moisture. ◨ CH 4ft/1.2m CS 3ft/1m **Z7–10**

Hakonechloa macra **'Aureola'**
Perennial grass that makes shaggy mounds of yellow leaves, flushed red in autumn – a good contrast with broad- or large-leaved plants. ◨ CH 14in/35cm CS 16in/40cm **Z5–9**

Heuchera micrantha **'Palace Purple'**
Large, almost metallic, purple leaves (*see p.15*) look handsome in a pot. Sprays of tiny white flowers appear in summer. ◨ CH to 18in/45cm CS 18in/45cm **Z4–8**

Hosta (Plantain lily)
Grown for their bold foliage, virtually all hostas are excellent for containers in shade (*see p.11*). Leaf sizes can vary greatly. Color varies, too; some leaves are variegated cream or yellow, others are chalky blue. Pale bell-shaped flowers are a late summer bonus. In pots, hostas tend to be less vulnerable to slug damage.
◨ CH to 2ft/60cm CS to 2ft/60cm **Z3–8**

Polystichum setiferum
(Soft shield fern)
Evergreen fern with fronds arranged in a shuttlecock. Delicate yet architectural; invaluable for winter interest.
◨ CH 18in/45cm CS 18in/45cm **Z6–9**

Sasa palmata f. *nebulosa*
Containers keep spreading bamboos within bounds. This one has handsome, broad leaves. Shelter it from winter wind to prevent them from browning. Divide plant once it fills its pot. ◨ CH 6ft/1.8m CS indefinite **Z6–10**

POLYSTICHUM SETIFERUM

MIXED DISPLAYS

Combining a range of plants in one large container produces eye-catching results but needs planning – all must enjoy the same conditions. They will also need careful management for a sustained display. On the other hand, soil mix in large containers is slower to dry out, so less water may be needed.

Argyranthemum (Marguerite)
A bright summer plant for large mixed pots. White, golden-eyed daisies appear continuously all summer. In most areas, overwinter in a greenhouse or conservatory, or buy new plants each year. There are many named marguerites, including 'Vancouver', with pink flowers fading buff; 'Mary Wootton', with pink flowers fading white; 'Jamaica Primrose', with yellow flowers. Evergreen, and can be trained as standards (*see p.60*). ⊠ CH to 28in/70cm CS to 28in/70cm **Z10–11**

Ballota pseudodictamnus
Forms attractive mounds of woolly gray-green leaves with whorls of pinkish white flowers in spring and early summer. Needs good drainage. ⊠ CH 18in/45cm CS 18in/45cm **Z7–9**

ARGYRANTHEMUM FRUTESCENS

Begonia semperflorens
Compact plants, sometimes with bronze leaves, are covered in small red, pink, or white flowers throughout summer. Will flower in shade. The Cocktail Series stands up well to wet weather. Best treated as an annual; do not put out young plants until all danger of frost has passed. ⊠ CH 8–12in/20–30cm CS 12in/30cm Min 55°F/13°C

Celosia argentea
(Cockscomb)
Plumes of bright featherlike flowers, often red or gold, stand well above the pale green leaves. The Fairy Fountains series includes pink, salmon, and pale yellow. Grow as an annual. ⊠ CH 16in/40cm CS 14in/35cm Annual

Diascia
Long-flowering perennials with several good choices for pots. Flowers range from pink to apricot to lilac. Not reliably hardy, but more likely to survive winter if given good drainage. *D. rigescens* has pink flowers on tall dense spikes and will trail and soften the edges of a container. 'Ruby Field' has deep pink, more open flower spikes. 'Lilac Belle' (*see p.53*) is good among silver-leaved plants such as ballota. ⊠ CH 6–12in/15–30cm CS to 20in/50cm **Z8–9**

GERBERA JAMESONII

Gerbera jamesonii
Vivid scarlet flowers appear from late spring to late summer. Selections such as the Pandora Series offer a wider color range, including cream, apricot, and lavender. Though perennial, treat as an annual in cold climates. ⊠ CH 12–18in/30–45cm CS 2ft/60cm Min 41°F/5°C

Helichrysum petiolare
Trailing stems of gray, woolly leaves are excellent in any mixed plantings in window-boxes and pots of all sizes. Can also be trained up stakes to form a dense pillar of foliage (*see p.63*). 'Limelight' has lime-green leaves. Loves baking in strong sun. Cut back shoots threatening to overwhelm other plants. Best treated as an annual. ⊠ CH to 12in/30cm CS 3ft/1m **Z10–11**

Heliotropium arborescens
(Heliotrope, Cherry pie)
Has wonderfully fragrant
violet-blue flowers in summer.
Place near a sitting area or
grow in a windowbox where
the scent will also waft into
indoor rooms. Usually treated
as an annual. ◘ CH 18in/45cm
CS 12–18in/30–45cm **Z11**

Hyacinthus orientalis
(Hyacinth)
Flower spikes of pink, white,
pale to deep blue, yellow, or
orange add fragrance and
color in early spring to
evergreen displays. After
foliage dies, bulbs can be
planted out in the garden.
◘◙ CH 8–12in/20–30cm
CS 4in/8cm **Z5–9**

Impatiens walleriana
(Impatiens)
Flowers throughout summer
even in shade; foliage can
vary from green to bronze.
Flowers may be double or
single, in many colors. The
Tempo Series includes violet,
lavender, orange, pink, and
red with several bicolors and
picotees. Treat as an annual,
and do not be tempted to put
out young plants until frosts
have ended.
◘ CH 18in/45cm CS
18in/45cm Min 50°F/10°C

Matthiola incana (Stocks)
Upright spikes of flowers
scent the air in late spring and
early summer. The Ten Week
Mixed have mainly double
flowers in crimson, pink,
lavender, purple, and white.
The Cinderella Series come in
similar shades but are shorter.
Usually grown as annuals.
◘ CH to 2ft/60cm
CS to 12in/30cm **Z7–8**

PLANTS FOR WINTER AND SPRING

You can create a year-round
display using tough, reliable
evergreens. Interplant them
with bulbs for spring. Later,
they will add structure to
summer bedding.

Bulbs For crocus, *Galanthus*
(snowdrops), iris, *Muscari*
(grape hyacinths), and
daffodils, see pp.74–75;
hyacinths, see left. Treat
bulbs as temporary, using
them for one year only
and planting them in the
garden, if possible, after
foliage dies.

Brassica oleracea
(Ornamental kale)
Highly colored ornamental
kale cultivars (*see pp.8, 39*)
put on a good display in
autumn and into winter.
Annuals; not recommended
for the table. ◘ CH and CS
to 18in/45cm Annual

Erica carnea
(Winter heath)
Evergreen heaths are good
in windowboxes where you
can see their winter flowers
from indoors. Flower in
purple, white, and pink;
some have gold foliage. Plant
in acidic soil mix. ◘ CH 6in/
15cm CS 18in/45cm **Z5–7**

Euonymus fortunei
Evergreen shrub forming
low mounds of leathery
leaves, often variegated. In
'Emerald 'n' Gold' the
leaves have yellow margins
tinged pink in winter.
◘◙◙ CH 16in/40cm
CS 2ft/60cm **Z5–9**

Hedera helix 'Goldheart'

Hebe pinguifolia 'Pagei'
Forms neat hummocks of
blue-green leaves with spikes
of white flowers in spring
and summer. ◘ CH 12in/
30cm CS 3ft/90cm **Z8–10**

Hedera helix (Ivy)
Variegated ivies, with leaves
marked with yellow, white,
or cream, brighten shaded
corners. Use small-leaved
ivies to trail over windowboxes, trimming regularly.
◙ CH to 10ft/3m
CS indefinite **Z5–10**

Vinca minor (Periwinkle)
Evergreen, with trailing
shoots studded with flowers
from spring to autumn.
Good for windowboxes and
tall pots. Colors range from
purple to pale blue and
white. Look for variegated
periwinkles with cream-
edged leaves. *V. major*
'Variegata' is attractive but
is an aggressive grower.
◘◙ CH 4–8in/10–20cm
CS 2ft/60cm **Z4–9**

Mimulus (Monkey flower)
Easily grown plants with
flowers produced throughout
late spring and summer. A
good range of bright colors,
especially yellows and reds, is
available among the bedding
mimulus. Treat as annuals. *M.
luteus* is a vigorous, spreading
perennial with red- or purple-
spotted yellow flowers. It is
likely to escape the container
and self-seed around the
garden. ▢▢ CH 12in/30cm
CS to 2ft/60cm **Z7–9**

Nicotiana (Flowering tobacco)
Flowers are often fragrant,
particularly in evening. The
Domino Series contains
attractive shades of rose and
salmon, as well as crimson,
pale green, and white. The
Starship Series stands up well
to poor weather, the plants
are shorter and good for
windowboxes, and the color
range includes white and lime
green. Grow as annuals,
putting plants out when frosts
are over. Flowers in light
shade; the trumpets often do
not open in full sun.
▢ CH to 18in/45cm
CS to 12in/30cm Annual

PELARGONIUM 'DOLLY VARDEN'

PETUNIA CARPET SERIES

Osteospermum
Long-flowering plant with
single daisy flowers, usually
white, pink, or yellow, from
late spring to autumn above
evergreen clumps of gray-
green leaves. Flowers open
only in full sun. 'Nairobi
Purple' is short and spreading
with purple flowers, white on
the reverse and with a black
center. 'Buttermilk' is
primrose yellow, bronze-
tinged on the reverse with a
bluish center. Overwinter in a
greenhouse or conservatory
or buy plantlets in spring.
▢ CH to 18in/45cm CS to
18in/45cm **Z10–11**

Pelargonium (Geranium)
One of the most traditional
plants for containers (*see
p.30*). The most suitable are
the zonal geraniums such as
'Dolly Varden' (*left*), and
miniatures such as 'Bird
Dancer'. There is a huge range
to choose from, with flowers
in shades of pink, red, mauve,
orange, and white, as well as
bicolors. Foliage may be
variegated. Trailing ivy-leaved
types are also good, especially
when planted along the edge

of a windowbox. Plants can
be protected in winter in a
greenhouse, conservatory, or
unheated room. ▢ CH to
16in/40cm CS 8–10in/
20–25cm Min 36°F/2°C

Petunia
One of the most popular
annuals for every type of
container. Modern hybrids are
as fail-safe as any container
plant can be. The Carpet
Series (*left*) is compact and
spreading – flower colors
include strong reds and
purples. Double-flowered
petunias are available; some
flowers have petals with white
stripes or margins, or may be
heavily veined. Wide range of
plants available in spring.
▢ CH 8–10in/20–25cm
CS 12in–3ft/30–90cm Annual

Salpiglossis sinuata
Annual with heavily-veined
flowers in interesting colors,
including bronze shades, from
summer to autumn. The
Casino Series plants are bushy
and compact with good all-
weather tolerance.
▢ CH 18in/45cm
CS 12in/30cm Annual

SALPIGLOSSIS SINUATA

SENECIO CINERARIA

Salvia
The fiery red annual
S. splendens provides one of
the brightest colors for
summer bedding. 'Scarlet
King' is compact and long
flowering. There are many
others to choose from; some
with softer colors prefer light
shade. The flower spikes of
S. coccinea are not as dense.
◪ CH to 16in/40cm
CS to 14in/35cm Annual

Senecio cineraria
(Dusty Miller)
The felted, silvery leaves make
bright-flowered neighbors
seem even brighter. Some
plants have lacy, almost white
foliage. Must have good
drainage. Overwinter in a
cold frame or greenhouse or
buy plants in spring. ◪ CH
12in/30cm CS 2ft/60cm Z8–10

Solenostemon scutellaroides
(Coleus)
Grown for its multicolored
green, cream, yellow, red,
and chocolate leaves. Often
treated as an annual, although
it can be taken indoors at the
end of summer. Plants in the
seed-grown Wizard Series are

compact; many excellent
cutting-grown selections are
also available. ◪ CH 8in/20cm
CS to 2ft/60cm Min 50°F/4°C

Stachys byzantina
(Lambs' ears)
Perennial that forms mats of
woolly, silver leaves. Blends
well with pink or blue flowers
(*see p.36*). Its own spikes of
lilac flowers appear in early
summer. A spreading plant, it
benefits from being planted
out in the garden after a
season in a container.
◪ CH to 18in/45cm
CS to 18in/45cm Z4–8

Tagetes (Marigold)
Easily grown annual with
yellow, orange, and
mahogany flowers from late
spring to early autumn.
Leaves are aromatic, almost
fernlike. The wide range
available includes plenty of
doubles. 'Naughty Marietta'
(*below*) has single flowers.
◪ CH 12–16in/30–40cm
CS 12in/30cm Annual

Tropaeolum (Nasturtium)
Colorful annual, excellent for
tumbling over the edges of

TAGETES 'NAUGHTY MARIETTA'

pots and windowboxes, with
flowers all summer and
autumn. The Alaska Series
has single flowers in orange,
mahogany, yellow, and cream
and cream-speckled leaves.
The Jewel Series has double
and semidouble flowers in
yellow, apricot, scarlet, or
crimson. 'Peach Melba' is a
creamy semidouble with
orange-red centers; it does
particularly well in containers.
All are easily grown from seed,
which can be sown directly
into the container where it is
to grow. Edible leaves and
flowers have a peppery taste.
◪ CH to 12in/30cm
CS to 18in/45cm Annual

Verbena
Good for the edges of large
containers. Some have a
spreading habit that combines
well with more upright
plants; others make more
upright, bushy plants by
themselves. Flowers continue
all summer and into autumn
and may be scented. There is
a good selection to choose
from, in shades of white,
peach, pink, red, and purple.
Bring indoors for winter;
usually grown as an annual.
◪ CH 12in/30cm CS 12–20in/
30–50cm Annual

Viola (Pansy)
Familiar pansy faces come in
a wide range of colors, sizes,
and markings. Perennial, but
usually grown as an annual or
biennial. Blooms in sun or
part shade, but plants last
longer out of hot summer
sun. Winter-flowering pansies
need plenty of light to bloom
through the season. Deadhead
regularly. ◪◪ CH to 10in/
25cm CS to 12in/30cm Z6–8

ROCK GARDEN PLANTS FOR TROUGHS

Most rock garden plants need a free-draining soil mix (*see p.55*). A top-dressing of coarse grit helps protect stems and lower leaves from rot or being splashed by soil mix. Choose plants that have similar requirements for sun or shade, and be ready to divide any that are invasive.

ANDROSACE CARNEA SUBSP. LAGGERI

Acaena (New Zealand burr)
Low, creeping evergreen perennials with dainty filigree foliage. 'Blue Haze' (*see p.53*) has blue-gray leaves with round, rust-colored burrs in mid to late summer. *A. microphylla* is smaller-growing; some plants have bronze leaves. ◨ CH to 6in/15cm CS 12in/30cm **Z6–8**

Achillea × lewisii 'King Edward'
Flat lemon flowerheads top mats of ferny, gray-green leaves from early to mid-summer (*see p.53*). ◨ CH 4–6in/8–12cm CS 10in/25cm **Z4–8**

Androsace carnea
(Rock jasmine)
An evergreen rock plant ideal for placing at the edge of a trough or sink. Clusters of small pink flowers form above rosettes of leaves in late spring. Subspecies *laggeri* has loose heads of deep pink flowers. Good drainage is essential. ◨ CH 2in/5cm CS 3–6in/8–15cm **Z4–7**

Arenaria balearica
A creeping perennial with tiny, shining evergreen leaves that form tight mats. Small star-shaped white flowers emerge at random throughout the summer. Ideal as a miniature alpine lawn in a trough in a shaded site. ◨ CH ¾in/2cm CS 12in/30cm **Z4–7**

Artemisia schmidtiana 'Nana'
Grow in a sunny trough, where it will make a silver carpet of fine silky leaves. An evergreen perennial that needs good drainage; add extra grit to the potting mix. ◨ CH 3in/8cm CS 12in/30cm **Z5–8**

Campanula (Bellflower)
Many of the small campanulas are suitable for troughs. The flowers, usually blue but sometimes white or lilac, appear in summer. *C. poscharskyana* has small blue bells and forms evergreen mats of bright green leaves; invasive and may need regular dividing. *C. raineri* is tiny and low-growing; it succeeds in shade. *C. carpatica* var. *turbinata* has fairly large upturned bells; 'Jewel' (*see p.53*) is compact with purple-blue flowers. Deadheading is needed to prevent faded, brown flowers from marring the display. A top-dressing of grit helps protect against slugs. ◨◨ CH to 6in/15cm CS 12–18in/30–45cm **Z4–8**

Crocus
Familiar harbingers of early spring with their goblet-shaped flowers. These need sun to open. *C. chrysanthus* types, such as 'Gipsy Girl' (*below*) are generally suitable for troughs with free-draining soil mix. 'Snow Bunting' is creamy white with pale gray feathering; 'Cream Beauty' is fragrant; and 'E.A. Bowles' is lemon with a bronze green base. ◨ CH 3in/8cm CS 2in/5cm **Z5–8**

CROCUS 'GIPSY GIRL'

CYCLAMEN COUM PEWTER GROUP

Cyclamen
The delightful white, pink, and carmine flowers of *C. coum* appear in late winter and early spring. The leaves, sometimes strikingly marked with silver patterns, can be almost as attractive as the flowers. The Pewter Group have almost entirely silver leaves. *C. hederifolium* flowers in autumn and can also have well-marked leaves. Cyclamen need gritty soil mix, with leaf mold or compost added, if possible. Plant tubers shallowly, just under the surface. ◪ CH 2–3in/5–8cm CS 4in/10cm **Z6–9**

Galanthus nivalis
(Snowdrop)
Charming late winter or early spring flowers for a natural-looking planting in partial shade. A raised trough enables you to appreciate them without getting on hands and knees. Many have single flowers, but the double 'Flore Pleno' is easy to grow. Divide clumps just after flowering, if necessary. ◪ CH 2–3in/5–8cm CS 2–2½in/5–6cm **Z3–9**

Gentiana sino-ornata
Brilliant blue trumpets give color from autumn into early winter. 'Kingfisher' (*below*) is similar. Plant in acidic soil mix. One of the easiest gentians to grow. ◪ CH 2–3in/5–8cm CS 6–12in/15–30cm **Z5–7**

Helianthemum (Rock rose)
Will bring color to troughs in the sun, with flowers in white, pink, red, or yellow, and silvery foliage. A spreading evergreen, it will trail over a trough's sides; some forms are upright. ◪ CH to 12in/30cm CS to 12in/30cm **Z6–8**

Iberis sempervirens
(Candytuft)
A particularly good scrambler for covering the sides of large troughs. The dark evergreen leaves make a useful mat of foliage all year. In late spring, the plant is covered by masses of small white flowers. ◪ CH 12in/30cm CS to 16in/40cm **Z5–9**

Iris histrioides
A small bulbous iris with mid- to dark blue flowers in

GENTIANA 'KINGFISHER'

NARCISSUS BULBOCODIUM

early spring. Ideal in a raised alpine trough, where the full beauty of the flowers can be appreciated more easily; could also be grown in a window-box. Keep as dry as possible in summer. ◪ CH 4–6in/10–15cm CS 2in/5cm **Z5–8**

Muscari armeniacum
(Grape hyacinth)
Easily grown bulb with short, dense spikes of tiny, round, blue bells in spring. Good in a large container or trough. Can produce a lot of foliage; if this becomes messy as the season wears on, it can be trimmed, unlike that of other bulbs, without detriment to the plant. Self-seeds readily. ◪ CH 8in/20cm CS 2in/5cm **Z4–8**

Narcissus bulbocodium
(Hoop-petticoat daffodil)
A small group of these delicate flowers (*above*) makes a charming addition to an alpine trough. Funnel-shaped trumpets produced in early spring. Grow in a sunny sheltered spot where the flowers will not be damaged by wind. ◪ CH 4–6in/10–15cm CS 2in/5cm **Z3–8**

ORIGANUM 'KENT BEAUTY'

Origanum 'Kent Beauty'

One of several decorative types of marjoram grown for their charming pink or green flowerheads. These will spill over the side of a trough from mid- to late summer. Leaves are aromatic but not edible. Other decorative marjorams include *O. amanum* and the more upright, purple-pink *O. laevigatum*. All need good drainage and will not survive excessively wet and cold winter conditions. Protect with a propped piece of glass. ◪ CH 4–8in/10–20cm CS to 12in/30cm **Z5–8**

Oxalis adenophylla

A delicate-looking perennial with gray-green leaves and purplish pink flowers in late spring. Flowers open only in good light. Can be tricky. ◪ CH 4in/10cm CS to 6in/15cm **Z6–8**

Primula auricula

(Auricula primrose)
Clusters of flowers, often with contrasting eyes or rings of white or gold, appear in late spring above evergreen rosettes of leaves (*see p.49*).

Flower colors include purple, red, blue, green, and yellow. Sometimes petals and leaves have a floury dusting. Add leaf mold or compost to a gritty planting mix. ◪ CH 8in/20cm CS 10in/25cm **Z3–8**

Saxifraga (Saxifrage)

Wide range of alpine plants, often forming mats of foliage. The flowers in spring come in delicate shades of pink, lemon, and white. For a challenge, try 'Tumbling Waters', with silvery-green leaves powdered white and clusters of white flowers; 'Southside Seedling' has sprays of tiny pink and white flowers; *S. burseriana* has lemon flowers and needs protection from very hot sun. Use gritty soil mix; top-dress with coarse grit. ◪ CH 18in/45cm CS 12in/30cm **Z3–9**

Scutellaria indica var. parvifolia (Skullcap)

Tolerates sun but a useful plant for a large alpine trough in partial shade. Lavender-blue tubular flowers are borne in summer above tufts of silver-gray leaves. ◪ CH 10in/25cm CS 12in/30cm **Z6–8**

OXALIS ADENOPHYLLA

SEMPERVIVUM TECTORUM

Sedum spathulifolium

An easily grown succulent with tiny rosettes of fleshy gray-green leaves, sometimes tinted purple. Spreads to form mats of foliage covered with bright yellow flowers in summer. 'Cape Blanco' (*see p.53*) has leaves heavily powdered with white. The leaves of 'Purpureum' have rich purple tones. ◪ CH 4in/10cm CS 2ft/60cm **Z5–9**

Sempervivum tectorum

(Hen and chicks)
Rosettes of succulent green, blue-green, or red-purple leaves make neat mats. Upright flowers shoot from their center in summer. Plants thrive in poor conditions. ◪ CH 6in/15cm CS to 20in/50cm **Z4–8**

Thymus (Thyme)

Low-growing thymes make attractive, aromatic trough plants. 'Doone Valley' forms mats of olive-green leaves splashed yellow, covered in summer with lavender-pink flowers. 'Silver Posie' makes a miniature bush with white-edged leaves. There are also gold-leaved thymes. All can be used in cooking, although plain green common thyme has best flavor. ◪ CH to 8in/20cm CS to 14in/35cm **Z4–9**

EDIBLE PLANTS

Most herbs make excellent container plants for the patio or windowsill. Vegetables and fruit need care with watering and feeding. Crops will be small but can be picked at the peak of freshness. Choose dwarf, fast-maturing vegetable cultivars, and feed with a quick-acting liquid fertilizer.

FRUIT AND VEGETABLES

Beans
Grow dwarf green beans in small spaces, putting 4 plants to a deep 12in/30cm pot. Runner beans can be put in half-barrels, trained up a tepee of 6ft/2m stakes. Keep well fed and watered.

Carrots
Feathery foliage is attractive in windowboxes. Choose short-rooted types.

Chili peppers
Need a really sunny, sheltered spot and long season to ripen. Several types available, giving dishes varying degrees of heat. 'Apache' makes a small, compact plant.

Lettuce
The frilly leaves of 'Lollo Rossa' (*right*) and 'Salad Bowl' types are decorative and can be picked a few at a time. Keep well watered and out of full sun.

Tomatoes
Give tomatoes in containers a sunny, sheltered site where they will develop most flavor. Trailing 'Sweet Million' is good in windowboxes.

Strawberries
Containers can produce a good crop in a sunny spot. Water well when fruit is swelling, and feed every 2 weeks with a high-potassium fertilizer. Replace plants every 2 years. Alpine strawberries are good in windowboxes and do well in light shade.

Citrus *See p.65*

HERBS

Basil
A tender annual that does especially well in pots in a warm, sheltered corner or on a sill. Pinch out shoot tips regularly to prevent plants becoming lankya and keep on the dry side. ◼ CH 12in–2ft/ 30–60cm CS 12in/30cm Annual

Chives
Easy to grow in sun or part shade. Mauve pompon flowers are an added attraction in early summer. ◼◼ CH to 2ft/60cm CS 4in/10cm **Z3–9**

Marjoram
Stems of aromatic leaves are topped by pretty pink flowers in early summer. 'Aureum' has yellow leaves. ◼ CH 12in/30cm CS 12in/30cm **Z5–9**

Mint
Invasive and best grown in its own pot. Various types have subtly differing flavors; those with variegated leaves often make more compact plants. Grow in shade, and provide plenty of moisture. ◼◼ CH to 2ft/60cm CS indefinite **Z3–7**

Parsley
The curly-leaved type is ornamental, but the flat-leaved type has a better flavor. Biennial. ◼◼ CH 12in/30cm CS 12in/30cm **Z5–8**

Sage
Gold- and purple-leaved sages taste good and look attractive mixed with other plants. Trim after flowering or in early spring to keep in shape. ◼ CH 18in/45cm CS 2ft/60cm **Z5–8**

See also **Thyme** (*opposite*) and **Bay** (*Laurus*) and **Rosemary** (*pp.66–67*).

LETTUCE 'LOLLO ROSSA'

INDEX

Page numbers in *italics*
indicate illustrations.

ACKNOWLEDGMENTS

Picture research Christine Rista

Special photography Peter Anderson

Illustrations Karen Cochrane

Index Hilary Bird

DK Publishing would like to thank:
All staff at the RHS, in particular Susanne Mitchell, Karen Wilson and Barbara Haynes at Vincent Square; Gerry Adamson for advice and assistance with the woodwork projects; Cuprinol Ltd (for wood preservative, p.33); Rein Ltd (for reinforcing fibres used in the cement trough, p.52); Stanley Tools Ltd.

American Horticultural Society
Visit AHS at www.ahs.org or call them at 1-800-777-7931, ext. 10. Membership benefits include *The American Gardener* magazine, free admission to flower shows, the free seed exchange, book services, and the Gardener's Information Service.

Photography
The publisher would also like to thank the following for their kind permission to reproduce their photographs:
(key: t=top, c=center, b=below, l=left, r=right)

DK Special Photography: Dave King 58bc
The Garden Picture Library: Linda Burgess 24; Mayer/ Le Scanff 6; J. S. Sira 11t; Friedrich Strauss 22br
John Glover: jacket back tc, 4bl, 5bl, 7, 9t, 10, 12l, 17, 21t, 22tr, 47b, designer Mark Anthony Walker
Harpur Garden Library: jacket back c, designer Martin Sacks 9b; designer Simon Fraser 12r
Andrew Lawson: jacket front tl and lct, 2, 8l, 11b, 14bl, 15br, 16, 19tr, 20
Clive Nichols Garden Pictures: jacket front r, 19br; Chenies Manor, Buckinghamshire 13b; Keukenhof, Holland 19tl; South View Nurseries, Hampshire 8r; Graham Strong 18
Photo Lamontagne: 30